BILL
GRIFFIN

The Meaning
of Wilderness

By Sigurd F. Olson

> *Listening Point*
>
> *The Lonely Land*
>
> *Of Time and Place*
>
> *Open Horizons*
>
> *Reflections from the North Country*
>
> *Runes of the North*
>
> *The Singing Wilderness*

By David Backes

> *A Wilderness Within:*
>
> > *The Life of Sigurd F. Olson*

Sigurd F. Olson

The Meaning

ESSENTIAL ARTICLES AND SPEECHES

of Wilderness

Edited and with

an Introduction by

David Backes

University of Minnesota Press   Minneapolis / London

Published by the University of Minnesota Press
111 Third Avenue South, Suite 290
Minneapolis, MN 55401-2520
http://www.upress.umn.edu

Library of Congress Cataloging-in-Publication Data

Olson, Sigurd F., 1899–1982
    The meaning of wilderness : essential articles and speeches /
Sigurd F. Olson ; edited and with an introduction by David Backes.
        p.   cm.
    ISBN 0-8166-3708-3
    1. Natural history—North America.   2. Philosophy of nature.
I. Backes, David.   II. Title.
    QH102 .O386 2001
    508.7—dc21
                                                            00-011869

Printed in the United States of America on acid-free paper

The University of Minnesota is an equal-opportunity educator and employer.

12 11 10 09 08 07 06 05 04 03 02 01   10 9 8 7 6 5 4 3 2 1

To the Listening Point Foundation, which works not only to preserve and protect Listening Point, the rugged and beautiful northern Minnesota lakeshore property that served as a getaway for Sigurd Olson, but also to promote Sigurd's philosophy and build upon his legacy in the field of wilderness education.

CONTENTS

Preface

SIGURD F. OLSON (1899–1982) is best known as the author of nine popular books that express the awe and wonder he found in nature. He is also remembered as a powerful speaker and environmental leader who became an icon of the wilderness preservation movement in the 1960s and 1970s. Sigurd's wilderness philosophy found strong support among national environmental leaders, federal land managers in the National Park Service and the U.S. Department of the Interior, and many thousands of ordinary citizens. Probably no other person since John Muir has received so much affectionate recognition in his lifetime as both a writer and environmental leader. Sigurd not only received the highest award in nature writing, the John Burroughs medal, but the top honors presented by four of the major American environmental groups: the Wilderness Society, the Sierra Club, the National Wildlife Federation, and the Izaak Walton League. He is the only person to have received more than two of these top environmental awards; only two of the more than sixty other Burroughs medal winners have received even one. George Marshall, who served as president of both the Wilderness Society and the Sierra Club, summed up the affection people felt for Sigurd in six words: "He made wilderness and life sing."

Sigurd's books are now available in paperback, but a major portion of his wilderness writing is relatively inaccessible, scattered in a number of magazines and obscure books over a period of nearly fifty years. Some of his speeches have never been published. This book gathers together his most important magazine articles and speeches about the meaning of wilderness; the goal is not only to make these important pieces more accessible but to show the development of Sigurd's philosophy during a span of half a century as a writer. The eighteen pieces chosen for this collection come from a variety of publications and from his papers at the Minnesota Historical Society in St. Paul. They are not by any means Sigurd's only articles and speeches about the meaning of wilderness, but there is a lot of redundancy among his entire body of work; he was, after all, writing and speaking to a number of distinct audiences, and so it is not unusual to find the same anecdotes and large chunks of passages in a handful of publications and manuscripts. The eighteen pieces selected cover all aspects of his philosophy, and with as little redundancy as possible.

When I read through Sigurd's articles and speeches to decide which ones to include in this book, the two key questions in my mind were (1) Does this piece illustrate an important aspect of his ideas about the meaning of wilderness? and (2) Is this the earliest of his articles and speeches to make this point? If the answer to each question was yes, I added the piece to this collection. If the answer to the second question was no, I excluded the piece, unless, as with several of them, I thought it contained something unique that would interest readers. Each of the eighteen articles and speeches is preceded by an introduction that provides context.

I am deeply grateful to my editor, Todd Orjala, copy editor Mary Keirstead, and the wonderful staff of the University of Minnesota Press. For suggestions and criticism, I would like to thank Gerald Killan, Clayton Russell, Paul Gruchow, Dan Philippon, and Don Scheese. For never-failing support and encouragement, I am especially grateful as always to Robert and Yvonne Olson, Sigurd T. Olson, my wife, Judi, and Heidi, Tim, Jenny, and Andrew.

Chronology of Sigurd Olson's Life

1899   Born in Humboldt Park, Chicago, on April 4.

1906   Family moves to Sister Bay, Wisconsin, on the rugged Door County peninsula.

1909   Family moves to Prentice, a logging town in north-central Wisconsin.

1912   Family moves to Ashland, Wisconsin, on the edge of Lake Superior.

1916–18   Sigurd attends Northland College in Ashland; works during the summers at a farm in Seeley, Wisconsin, owned by Soren Uhrenholdt.

1918–20   Sigurd attends the University of Wisconsin in Madison, and earns undergraduate degree in agriculture.

1920–22   Sigurd teaches animal husbandry, agricultural botany, and geology in the high schools of the neighboring northern Minnesota towns of Nashwauk and Keewatin.

1921   Sigurd takes his first canoe trip in June; marries Elizabeth Dorothy Uhrenholdt on August 8. Their honeymoon is a three-week canoe trip. Eight days before the wedding, on July 31, the *Milwaukee Journal* publishes Sigurd's first article, an account of his June canoe trip.

1922 Sigurd starts graduate program in geology at the University of Wisconsin in Madison; Elizabeth helps with finances by teaching elementary school in Hayward, Wisconsin.

1923 In January Elizabeth learns she is pregnant; Sigurd drops out of school and lands a job teaching high school biology in Ely, Minnesota, at the edge of the canoe country wilderness. They move there in February. During the summer, Sigurd finds work as a canoe trip guide, which he continues doing every summer throughout the 1920s. Sigurd and Elizabeth become parents on September 15, when Sigurd Thorne Olson is born.

1925 Robert Keith Olson is born on December 23. Sigurd is involved in the first battle over the canoe country wilderness, a conflict over proposals to build roads into previously inaccessible areas.

1926 In September the U.S. Secretary of Agriculture ends the current canoe country conflict by allowing two major roads to be built, and by creating three wilderness areas within Superior National Forest. Meanwhile, Sigurd begins splitting his teaching duties between Ely High School and Ely Junior College. At the junior college, he teaches animal biology and human physiology.

1927 In November *Field and Stream* publishes Sigurd's first magazine article, "Fishin' Jewelry."

1929 Sigurd and two other men found the Border Lakes Outfitting Co. As manager, Sigurd spends less of his time guiding than in the past. He manages the company until the mid-1940s and maintains partial ownership until 1951.

1931–32   In the fall of 1931, the Olsons move to Champaign, Illinois, so Sigurd can earn a master's degree in zoology at the University of Illinois. Sigurd works under Victor Shelford, the nation's leading animal ecologist. He earns his degree in June 1932, after completing a thesis—the first of its kind—on the timber wolf. The Olsons move back to Ely, and Sigurd begins teaching full-time at Ely Junior College.

1932   In May and June *Sports Afield* publishes Sigurd's two-part article "Search for the Wild," his first article fully devoted to wilderness philosophy.

1936   Sigurd becomes dean of Ely Junior College.

1938   In September *American Forests* publishes Sigurd's article "Why Wilderness?" Superior National Forest's three wilderness areas, recently enlarged, are renamed the Superior Roadless Areas.

1941   Sigurd begins a syndicated newspaper column, "America Out of Doors." It lasts until 1944, and then, like many syndicated columns of the time, it dies as government wartime restrictions on newsprint force newspapers to cut back.

1945   In June Sigurd heads to Europe for a year as a civilian employee of the army. He teaches GIs waiting to be shipped back to America and is an official observer at the Nuremberg trials.

1947   Sigurd resigns as dean of Ely Junior College to devote full time to his writing.

1948–49   Sigurd spearheads the fight to ban airplanes from the wilderness canoe country near his home. It is

a precedent-setting, successful battle and brings
Sigurd national recognition in conservation circles.

1951   Sigurd becomes vice president of the National
Parks Association.

1953   Sigurd becomes president of the National Parks
Association.

1955   The year begins with Sigurd signing his first book
contract, with Alfred A. Knopf. In the summer,
Sigurd and a group of prominent Canadian friends
spend several weeks paddling the wild Churchill
River in Saskatchewan, one of a handful of rugged
trips they would take together.

1956   *The Singing Wilderness* is published in April, shortly
after Sigurd's fifty-seventh birthday. It becomes
a *New York Times* bestseller. In the summer the
Wilderness Society elects Sigurd to its governing
council. Sigurd is among the conservation leaders
working on drafts of a bill to establish a national
wilderness preservation system.

1958   *Listening Point* is published; the Superior Roadless
Areas are renamed the Boundary Waters Canoe
Area.

1959   Sigurd resigns as president of the National Parks
Association and joins the advisory board of the
National Park Service. He remains on the board
until 1966.

1961   *The Lonely Land* is published.

1962   Sigurd becomes a consultant on wilderness and
national park matters for Secretary of the Interior
Stewart Udall.

1963   *Runes of the North* is published; Sigurd becomes
vice president of the Wilderness Society.

1964   In July sixty-five-year-old Sigurd embarks on his
        last major canoe expedition, a voyage from Lake
        Winnipeg to Hudson Bay along the Nelson and
        Hayes Rivers. In September President Lyndon B.
        Johnson signs the Wilderness Act, establishing the
        national wilderness preservation system.

1965   Sigurd is part of a National Park Service task force
        that recommends preserving nearly eighty million
        acres of land in Alaska. Fearing a political firestorm,
        the agency buries the report, but the work behind
        it ultimately bears fruit in the Alaska National
        Interest Lands and Conservation Act of 1980.

1968   Sigurd becomes president of the Wilderness Society.
        In November he suffers a major heart attack dur-
        ing the society's annual meeting at Sanibel Island,
        Florida.

1969   *Open Horizons* and *The Hidden Forest* are
        published.

1971   Sigurd resigns as president of the Wilderness So-
        ciety, citing his health and desire to write. President
        Richard M. Nixon signs into law the act establishing
        Voyageurs National Park in northern Minnesota;
        Sigurd had played an important role as an advocate
        of the park since the early 1960s, and he also gave
        the park its name. Also in 1971, a new elementary
        school in the Minneapolis suburb of Golden Valley
        is named after Sigurd.

1972   *Wilderness Days* is published; the Sigurd Olson En-
        vironmental Institute is established at Northland
        College in Ashland, Wisconsin.

1974   The highest honor in nature writing, the John
        Burroughs Medal, is presented to Sigurd.

1976   *Reflections from the North Country* is published.

1977   Sigurd is hanged in effigy in his hometown of Ely, Minnesota, during debates about the status of the Boundary Waters Canoe Area.

1978   President Jimmy Carter signs the law granting full wilderness status to the Boundary Waters Canoe Area Wilderness, more than fifty years after Sigurd's first efforts to protect it.

1979   In December Sigurd undergoes successful surgery for colon cancer. However, he never fully regains his strength.

1982   On January 13 Sigurd dies of a heart attack while showshoeing near his home. *Of Time and Place* is published.

1994   Elizabeth Olson dies of heart failure on August 23, at the age of ninety-six.

1998   The Listening Point Foundation is established.

Introduction

David Backes

Sigurd olson was not the first American to discuss the spiritual values of wilderness, nor was he the most scholarly. He simply was the most beloved wilderness advocate of his generation.

Something in his bearing had a strong effect on people. It was a combination of gracefulness, poise, confidence, and an engaging voice. His wife, Elizabeth, recalled times when Sigurd entered a room and everyone rose as if on cue, heads straining to see him. And when he spoke, people hung on to his words.

"Sig conveyed a religious fervor and a depth of conviction that no one else I know succeeded in generating," said former Minnesota Governor Elmer L. Andersen. "Others could win adherence; he produced disciples."[1]

Not surprisingly, this disciple producer was the son of a minister, and nearly became a missionary himself. Born in Chicago on April 4, 1899, Sigurd was the second of three sons raised by the Reverend Lawrence and Ida May Olson, Swedish immigrants who met and married in the United States. Sigurd's parents were Swedish Baptists, a branch of the Baptist faith toughened by decades of persecution in Sweden.

Sigurd's mother was a devout Swedish Baptist who stood firmly against drinking and dancing, but she was sweet and generally cheerful, and had a good sense of humor. Sigurd's father, on the other hand, was a fire-and-brimstone preaching fundamentalist who led antialcohol campaigns and told his sons to turn their heads whenever they passed a Catholic church. Lawrence—or L.J., as he was called—was also a stern, grim man, very reserved and formal. He had little sympathy for amusements. One time he discovered that Sigurd and his older brother, Kenneth, had saved up money and bought a chess set. L.J. grabbed it away from them and threw it into the fire.

Whether it was because of this background or in spite of it, as a young adult Sigurd nearly became a missionary. While attending the University of Wisconsin in Madison at the end of World War I, he became chapter president of the Student Volunteers, American Protestantism's most important missionary organization. But during this same period, doubts about his calling and his faith assailed him. The night before he was to publicly make his commitment to the missionary life he climbed to the roof of the YMCA building where he lived, looked out over Lake Mendota and up at the stars, and struggled with his conscience. He decided that his fascination with the missions had more to do with his interest in visiting the wild places of the world than with saving souls. When he came down from the roof the next morning, he resigned from the organization, and in effect also broke from his Baptist faith.

For years afterward, he was obsessed with what he called his search for meaning. To lose belief in the dogma of his parents' church was one thing, but to lose faith in the idea of a mission or a calling in life cut deeply into his psyche. "For years I went on getting more bitter and disillusioned all of the time," he recalled in his journal on January 14, 1930. His only hope for happiness was to recover a sense of mission. Before that could happen, however, he needed to regain his faith in a greater power.

He found it, of course, in nature. As a young child he began to sense what he would later call "the singing wilderness." His family moved from Chicago to several small Wisconsin towns during his youth, and he formed a passionate, visceral connection to the natural world. But the defining moment came to him as a young man during the early 1920s, while on a canoe trip into the western portion of Ontario's Quetico Provincial Park. By then Sigurd was married, had the first of his two sons, and lived in the northern Minnesota city of Ely at the edge of what is now called the Boundary Waters Canoe Area Wilderness, which borders the Quetico. He taught biology at the local high school, and then at Ely Junior College, where he later became dean. During summers he made extra money and satisfied his craving for the outdoors by working as a guide for a local outfitting company. One summer evening, camped on an island in Robinson Lake, Sigurd got into his canoe after dinner and paddled to the nearby eastern shore of the lake where there was a peak with a gorgeous view of the wilderness to the west. Sigurd climbed to the top in time to watch the sunset and experienced a deep communion with nature. Years later, he described it in his first book, *The Singing Wilderness,* in a passage that set the tone not only for that book but for the message he brought in all of his books and speeches:

> As I watched and listened, I became conscious of the slow, steady hum of millions of insects and through it the calling of the whitethroats and the violin notes of the hermit thrushes. But it all seemed very vague from that height and very far away, and gradually they merged one with another, blending in a great enveloping softness of sound no louder, it seemed, than my breathing.
>
> The sun was trembling now on the edge of the ridge. It was alive, almost fluid and pulsating, and as I watched it sink I thought that I could feel the earth turning from it, actually feel its rotation. Over all was the silence of the wilderness, that sense of oneness which comes only when there are no distracting sights or sounds, when we listen with inward ears and see with inward eyes, when we feel and are aware with our entire beings rather than our senses. I thought as I sat there of the

ancient admonition "Be still and know that I am God," and
knew that without stillness there can be no knowing, without
divorcement from outside influences man cannot know what
spirit means.[2]

During his summers as a canoe country guide Sigurd noticed
how often his clients, too, were transformed over the course of
a canoe trip. The exterior, formal layers of their business personas were gradually peeled away, and they would begin to
laugh and sing and experience a deep peace. Like Sigurd, they
became reconnected to the grand, eternal mystery of creation.

Sigurd came to believe his mission in life was to share with
others what he had found in the wilderness, and to help lead
the fight to preserve what he called "a few last entrenchments
of the spirit."[3] Science, technology, and materialism were turning many people away from the religious truths and practices
that had given spiritual sustenance, and offered nothing in their
place. The result was a widespread, if often vague, discontent,
partially hidden underneath fast-paced lives, yet also fed by
that same fast pace that left little time for reflection. Sigurd
knew that the silence and the solitude and the noncivilized
surroundings of wilderness provide a physical context in which
people can more easily rediscover their inner selves. Just as important, wilderness gives people a chance to feel the presence
of a universal power that science can never explain but that
brings meaning to their lives. "Wilderness offers [a] sense of
cosmic purpose if we open our hearts and minds to its possibilities," he said at a national conference in 1965:

> It may come in . . . burning instants of truth when everything
> stands clear. It may come as a slow realization after long peri-
> ods of waiting. Whenever it comes, life is suddenly illumined,
> beautiful, and transcendent, and we are filled with awe and
> happiness.[4]

Sigurd spread his philosophy in nine books, in more than a
hundred magazine articles, in a syndicated newspaper column,
and in countless speeches and conversations across the United

States and Canada. By the 1970s he was a beloved environmental figurehead whose name and image evoked strong feelings. Often photographed with a pipe in his hand and a warm, reflective expression on his weathered face, he was not just a hero but an icon. His books were read on public radio, his portrait was taken by Alfred Eisenstaedt for *Life* magazine, and awards almost routinely came his way. "To many of us," said Sierra Club president Edgar Wayburn, "he is the personification of the wilderness defender."[5]

Today, nearly twenty years after Sigurd's death, and at the beginning of a new millennium, he is still revered by many, but their numbers are fewer, and they are located primarily in Minnesota and Wisconsin. Yet the recent publication of his biography and the first republication of his books in paperback format have sparked a resurgence of interest in this one-time wilderness icon. Now there is the potential for a new generation of those who love wild places to read Sigurd's works for the first time.

Why should they? It must be admitted, there are a couple of strikes against Sigurd's writing in the twenty-first century. First, anyone who reads his works today must find it at least initially jarring to see Sigurd's constant use of masculine pronouns, and some may raise questions about race and class. Second, those who are deeply aware of current debates about the meaning of wilderness might wonder if Sigurd's ideas are still relevant.

The times clearly have changed since Sigurd wrote his books. Wilderness writers of his generation routinely used masculine pronouns. Nearly all of Sigurd's writing from the 1920s through the 1940s was published by magazines directed primarily to men. The editors of such publications as *Sports Afield, Field and Stream,* and *Outdoor Life* rejected articles of his that they felt contained too much philosophy and not enough action. While there is no evidence that he was ever told to use masculine pronouns, it was the expected practice, and so common he probably never even thought about it. After several decades of writing this way, it is not surprising that he continued to do so.

Even so, Sigurd believed that women in general were more

likely to understand and appreciate his essays than the men of his time, whom he thought were too action-oriented.[6] And regardless of the fact that women rarely appeared in his wilderness essays, he certainly believed they belonged in the wilderness. He often worked with the Girl Scouts in Ely, and he frequently outfitted canoe parties of women. Also, he *did* on at least one occasion write an article meant to combat the idea that women should stay out of the wilderness. Written for a syndicated newspaper outdoor series in 1937, it was called "Can Women Take Canoe Trips?"[7]

Some may raise related issues of race and class. Again, Sigurd must be placed in the context of his times—his audiences were almost entirely white, and middle class or higher. Even today it must be admitted that for whatever reasons, minorities are underrepresented among any random selection of people who visit wilderness areas or read nature essays. The only times Sigurd ever used the words "race" or "racial" in his writings he used the terms in the context of "the human race," and in that sense he was inclusive of all people. In general, he wrote favorably of, and even romanticized, the one minority group he ever mentioned, Native Americans. He also bemoaned the loss of Native American culture and advocated giving Indians "the right to work out their own destiny in a creative way that would build rather than destroy not only them, but also the land to which they belong."[8]

As for class, it is still true to this day that people who visit wilderness areas or read nature essays are more likely than the average citizen to have an education beyond a bachelor's degree. Wilderness users are primarily among the educated elite, rather than the economic elite, while readers of nature essays are probably among the elite in both categories. When Sigurd worked as a guide, his clients were primarily white-collar professionals from urban areas. As a conservationist, he worked primarily among the educated and economic elite. Yet once again, whenever Sigurd wrote about people who were not among the social elite, he wrote favorably and even romanticized them.

Among his most cherished role models were farmers, loggers, guides, and trappers, including a man who had served time for murder (and later was pardoned). And his strong support of hunting put him at odds with many of the social elite of his era, and at times with his conservation colleagues.

It is unfair, then, to judge harshly Sigurd's works on grounds of sex, race, or class. But does he have anything to say that can still contribute to today's discussions about the meaning of wilderness? Those inclined to answer no might make the following charges, all of which I have encountered occasionally (from scholars only, I might add) during the years I have spent writing and speaking about him:

> His knowledge of ecology rests on a hopelessly dated perspective, and so his ecological arguments in favor of wilderness preservation are flawed.
>
> He propounds a simplistic antimodernism in which nature "untouched by man" is good, and urban civilization is bad.
>
> He is anthropocentric.
>
> He is unoriginal.

It is true that Sigurd's understanding of ecology is dated. As a graduate student at the University of Illinois in the early 1930s, Sigurd learned an organismic ecological perspective that lent itself to inductive reasoning rather than to the reductive methods of modern science. He learned that the whole is greater than the sum of the parts, and that an ecosystem can reach a point in its development—the climax community—where change is minimal, and harmony reigns supreme. In fact, however, the organismic perspective became outdated during his lifetime. By World War II ecological research had grown far more reductive, increasingly relying upon quantitative analysis and rigorous scientific methodology. In the years since Sigurd's death in 1982, this trend, along with the integration of applied biology, population biology, and ecology, has led to the new discipline of conservation biology. With its emphasis on preserving ecosystems and biodiversity, conservation biology provides the dominant perspective of today's wilderness movement.

Sigurd's key arguments on behalf of wilderness do not depend on his organismic perspective, so even if his ecological views are considered naive by today's experts, that does not invalidate his arguments. And one aspect of his understanding of ecosystems may add an important minority voice to today's discussions about the meaning of wilderness. The organismic perspective leads to the view that nature is best managed by letting it manage itself. "As a practicing ecologist, I feel strongly about letting nature take its course," Sigurd wrote to a U.S. Forest Service official in 1971.[9] And while he understood the reasons for actively managing ecosystems, he lamented the loss of wildness—both actual and perceived—that resulted, as he made clear in this passage from *Runes of the North*:

> There was a movement below me, and three caribou appeared in a narrow gully leading to my resting place among the rocks. The wind was in my favor and I froze, waiting. The first was a beautiful bull with an enormous rack; the others, cows. Then I saw the orange ribbons hanging from their ears and somehow for me the sense of the old north was gone. No longer were they of the ancient tundra, of the days of arrows and spears. These animals were managed, part of a scientific research project, specimens in the laboratory of their range.
>
> I felt much the same as when I found a band on a wild mallard I had shot, watched ducklings which had been colored by injections of dye into the eggs from which they came, or saw a grizzly in the mountains of the west with an orange spot on its rump and a transistor inside. Must this, I thought, be the fate of all wild creatures left to us; must we in our need of knowledge mark and record the movements of all free, living things to learn their secrets? Had we now reached a point in our conquest of the earth when, because of our expanding population and human depredations, there was no longer an opportunity for other forms to live undisturbed?[10]

While the average person likely takes Sigurd's sentiment about leaving nature alone as a matter of course, it has become a minority view among those most involved in shaping environmental philosophy and policy. Even radical environmentalism, as Jack Turner demonstrates in one of the recent volumes about current wilderness debates, has succumbed to conservation biology's perspective in which control over nature is assumed to be the only way to preserve biodiversity. It is a perspective that asks us to trust scientific experts and technology. The true radical view today is Sigurd's preference to leave nature alone, and, as Turner says, it is supported by the philosophical implications of the new and rapidly growing body of writings on chaos theory: "What emerges from the recent work on chaos and complexity is the final dismemberment of the ideology of the world as machine. In its place is the view of the world characterized by wildness, vitality, and freedom."[11] In a world of dynamic systems marked by chaos and complexity, quantitative prediction is beyond the limits of science, and so, therefore, is control. Turner writes:

> What happens to the rationality of managing species and ecosystems without accurate prediction and control? If the subsystems of an ecosystem (from vascular flows to genetic drift plus all the natural disturbances to ecosystems—weather, fire, wind, earthquakes, avalanches), if all these exhibit chaotic and complex behavior, and this behavior does not allow quantitative predictions, then isn't "ecosystems management" a bit of a sham and isn't the management of grizzlies and wolves at best a travesty? Why don't we just can the talk of health and integrity and admit, honestly, that it's just public policy? Why don't we just fire the Inter Agency Grizzly Team forthwith and let them do something useful?[12]

The second charge that those who would dismiss Sigurd's relevance to current wilderness discussions might make is that he propounds a simplistic antimodernism in which nature "untouched by man" is good, and urban civilization is bad. They might even quote from one of the articles included in this volume. In "Reflections of a Guide," for example, Sigurd writes: "He realizes that civilization has cramped his spirit too long in its efforts to mold and make him live his life like millions of other human machines." They might further argue that Sigurd's writings show a dualistic perspective in which humans are not part of the natural world. And they might quote environmental historian William Cronon, who, in a critique of the wilderness movement that started a firestorm of debate, wrote that

> the most troubling cultural baggage that accompanies the celebration of wilderness has less to do with remote rain forests and peoples than with the ways we think about ourselves. . . . Idealizing a distant wilderness too often means not idealizing the environment in which we actually live, the landscape that for better or worse we call home. Most of our serious environmental problems start right here, at home, and if we are to solve those problems, we need an environmental ethic that will tell us as much about *using* nature as about *not* using it. The wilderness dualism tends to cast any use as *ab*-use, and thereby denies us a middle ground in which responsible use and non-use might attain some kind of balanced, sustainable relationship. . . . The middle ground is where we actually live. . . .
>
> Indeed, my principal objection to wilderness is that it may teach us to be dismissive or even contemptuous of such humble places and experiences [as the wildness in our own backyards].[13]

It is easy, as I said earlier, to find antimodern statements in Sigurd's writings. He made some strong negative statements about large cities and the direction of modern society. It also is not hard to find evidence of a human/nature dualism in his works. But it is easy to make too much of this. Taken as a whole, Sigurd's life and works show beyond a doubt that he did *not* simplistically view modern civilization as bad and pris-

tine wilderness as the only source of goodness. He devoted his
life to the belief that they are necessary *complements to each
other,* that neither can be fully understood or appreciated without the other. As he told wilderness activists and scholars in
April 1961, in a speech included in this volume,

> We are trying to bridge the gap between our old racial wis-
> dom, our old primeval consciousness, the old verities, and the
> strange, conflicting ideologies and beliefs of the new era of
> technology. One of the most vital tasks of modern man is to
> bridge this gap. . . . None of us is naive enough to want to give
> up what technology has brought or to evade the challenges
> now before us. This too is a frontier, not only of the mind but
> of the physical world. Somehow we must make the adjustment
> and bring both ways of life together. If man can do this, if he
> can span past and present, then he can face the future with
> confidence.[14]

Sigurd's philosophy is about balance, in fact a balance very
compatible with William Cronon's comments. Sigurd is forever
identified with wilderness, and for good reason, but many of his
essays are about the kind of backyard and neighborhood wildness Cronon says is underappreciated. He wrote about building
a stone wall in his yard, about transplanting a scrub oak, about
ice-skating down a lake next to town in the midst of a blaze of
northern lights, about the fate of migrating birds in his neighborhood after a sudden spring snowstorm. He also wrote a series of
essays based on a piece of property he called Listening Point,
located near Ely on a lake with resorts, permanent homes, and
other cabins. The essays show his struggles over where to put
the cabin, over the question of whether and how to build a road
into his property, and over other ordinary issues of managing a
cherished piece of land. It was in his book *Listening Point* that
he chastised himself for his initial anger when a moment of
wilderness-type silence was disturbed by the sound of a train's
whistle:

Without that long lonesome wail and the culture that had produced it, many things would not be mine—recordings of the world's finest music, books holding the philosophy, the dreams and hopes of all mankind, a car that took me swiftly to the point whenever I felt the need. All these things and countless others civilization had given me, and I must never again forget that because of the wonders it had wrought this richness now was mine. . . . The very presence of the railroad and highway over the ridges to the south gave new significance to wilderness, to solitude and the entire concept of Listening Point.[15]

Sigurd *found* that middle ground Cronon says is lacking among wilderness advocates. He found it, and he wrote about it, and in doing so, he demonstrated the kind of environmental ethic Cronon says is necessary, an ethic "that will tell us as much about *using* nature as about *not* using it." To Sigurd, land-use issues are not always black and white; knowledge of context is essential. His book *Listening Point,* in particular, illustrates the middle-ground land ethic of a man who believed that people find the deepest fulfillment when—whether in the wilderness or in their backyard—they do simple things that are in harmony with their surroundings and with their evolutionary heritage as humans.

The third charge, that of anthropocentrism, is half right. There is plenty of evidence showing that Sigurd believed mankind is the highest product of evolution. Sigurd, along with the evolutionary humanists such as Julian Huxley and Lewis Mumford, believed the development of culture distinguished mankind from other animals. To Sigurd, the development of love, in particular, was most important. "Granted," he wrote, "that creatures other than man show love and feeling not only for their young but for each other, only in man has it progressed to where it is a major force in his development and culture." Phrased another way, "Man has come from the same earth stuff as other creatures, but through the accident of evolutional development we are the fortunate ones."[16]

Love was the most important element in Sigurd's environmentalism. "There can be no real, lasting land ethic without love," he said. But his idea of love went beyond humans to include all living things. "What civilization needs today," he wrote, "is a culture of sensitivity and tolerance and an abiding love of all creatures including mankind."[17] And wilderness, he believed, played an important role in producing this biocentric perspective. In experiencing a high degree of *silence* and *solitude* amid *noncivilized surroundings,* wilderness visitors can easily reconnect to their evolutionary heritage as humans, and by sensing the grandeur of the eternal mystery of creation and their own participation in this mystery—their own connectedness to all things—they will come to sense the *sacredness* of all creation. If, as Sigurd believed, evolution is proceeding toward union with God—what he and others called the emergent God—and if, as he also believed, individual spiritual growth plays an essential role in this evolutionary process, then a wilderness experience can be considered a sacramental experience, of benefit not just to the individual or to humanity at large but to all of creation. Sigurd's philosophy may start with some assumptions identified with anthropocentrism, but it leads to a biocentric conclusion.

The final issue is that of originality. On one level, it is very difficult to respond to someone asking what Sigurd had to say that was original. When is anyone truly original? But rather than get into a deep philosophical argument over this, let me make it easier by agreeing that many of Sigurd's ideas about the meaning of wilderness are commonplace. At the same time, the totality of his wilderness philosophy—theology, really, because it was deeply connected with his beliefs about the nature of God—is quite different from the typical philosophy expressed by other leading wilderness activists and writers, either of his time or of today. One part of his wilderness theology owes a debt to Aldous and Julian Huxley, Lewis Mumford, Pierre Lecomte du Noüy, and Pierre Teilhard de Chardin. This part is, as described earlier, the idea that evolution is proceeding along a spiritual path toward union with God. He combined this with his belief that our instincts *demand* that we seek contact with nature. "We all have a pronounced streak of the primitive set deep within us," he wrote in a 1928 article included in this volume, "an instinctive longing that compels us to leave the confines of civilization and bury ourselves periodically in the most inaccessible spots we can penetrate."[18] This statement, published in *Field and Stream,* was his first description of what he came to call "racial memory": the idea that humans have a biological attachment to nature that arises from our long evolutionary heritage. Again, this was not a new idea, but he gave far more emphasis to it than did any other leading wilderness movement thinker or nature writer. The theory of racial memory provided a biological underpinning to his ideas about the spiritual values of wilderness. "Because man's subconscious is steeped in the primitive," he said, "looking to the wilderness actually means a coming home to him," and the impact of traveling into it is so strong that "reactions are automatically set in motion that bring in their train an uplift of the spirit." Wilderness visitors may experience "burning instants of truth when everything stands clear" or may realize life's purpose "after long periods of waiting." In other words, by returning to our biological roots in the wilderness, we can more easily open ourselves to spiritual experience and come to know our true selves.[19]

While the theory of racial memory has ties to the romantics and primitivists, and to the "collective unconscious" described by psychologist Carl Jung, it did not receive much scholarly attention or support during Sigurd's lifetime. In recent years, however, this key aspect of Sigurd's wilderness theology has become the cornerstone of the emerging scholarly discipline of evolutionary psychology. And the researchers are demonstrating what Sigurd asserted: ten thousand years of agriculture and the brief era of industrialized civilization cannot significantly change millions of years of evolutionary design and behavior.[20] We are, in essence, Pleistocene creatures who cannot be fully human unless we have regular contact with the wild.

So, while the various pieces of Sigurd's philosophy might not be particularly original, his incorporation of the theory of racial memory with a spiritual perspective steeped in evolutionary humanism gives his ideas about the meaning of wilderness a power and uniqueness that is not only relevant in the twenty-first century, but needed. At the same time, to focus too closely on the question of Sigurd's originality, as scholars are wont to do, is really to miss the point. A theology or a philosophy is worthless if it cannot be expressed in a way that touches people's hearts. Sigurd wanted to bring his message of wilderness salvation to people who would never think of reading Teilhard de Chardin or Lewis Mumford or even a more popular but still intellectual writer such as Loren Eiseley. In August 1960, for example, he said in a note to himself, "I must bridge the gap between Eiseley and my audience of common people, the non-intellectuals . . . who feel deeply but are groping for ideas."[21] And he found tremendous success. Sigurd's collected papers at the Minnesota Historical Society are full of letters from men and women who said they had finally found someone who had put into words the feelings they had experienced in the outdoors, either in their backyards or in the wilderness. Sigurd's special gift was his ability to express his deep message about the spiritual values of nature by writing about simple things—the sound of wings over a marsh, the smell of a bog, the memories stirred by a campfire, the movement of a canoe—in a way that captured the emotions they stirred. Sigurd Olson may not have become the Baptist minister his father once hoped for, but a missionary he was, a wilderness evangelist with legions of followers. He was an apostle of awe, a witness for wonder, and an icon of the modern wilderness movement whose words will continue to stir hearts and souls for generations to come.

NOTES

1. Quoted in Robert B. Oetting, "Sigurd Olson, Environmentalist," *Naturalist,* autumn 1981.

2. Sigurd F. Olson, *The Singing Wilderness* (New York: Alfred A. Knopf, 1956), 130–31.

3. Sigurd Olson, "The Supernatural Instinct," unpublished manuscript dated Dec. 26, 1933. The Sigurd Olson Papers are at the Minnesota Historical Society in St. Paul.

4. Sigurd F. Olson, "The Spiritual Need," in Bruce M. Kilgore, ed., *Wilderness in a Changing World* (San Francisco: Sierra Club, 1966), 218.

5. Wayburn said this on April 8, 1972, while presenting Olson with an honorary life membership in the Sierra Club, the thirty-fifth such award in the club's eighty years of existence.

6. See, for example, his journal entry of April 25, 1939, in which he discussed seeking a female literary agent to replace the men he had been unhappy with: "I am of the opinion that no man dealing with blood and thunder stuff will ever want to take care of my stuff, that it takes a woman's greater sensitiveness to understand what it is I am trying to do. Burroughs found the same thing, that women were his greatest audience, that men as a rule were too thick skinned to understand or appreciate what he did."

7. The manuscript is in the Olson Papers. It was one of his first submissions to the "America Out of Doors" series. At that time the column was written by a rotating crew of well-known outdoor writers, including Ozark Ripley, Buell Patterson, Harold Hollis, Cal Johnson, and Bob Lincoln. In 1941 Sigurd would become the sole writer of the column, which folded in 1944, a victim of wartime newsprint restrictions.

8. Sigurd F. Olson, *Runes of the North* (New York: Alfred A. Knopf, 1963), 155.

9. Olson to Supervisor, Superior National Forest, June 23, 1971.

10. Olson, *Runes,* 176–77.

11. Jack Turner, "The Quality of Wildness: Preservation, Control, and Freedom." In David Clarke Burks, ed., *Place of the Wild* (Washington, D.C.: Island Press, 1994), 186.

12. Ibid., 186–87.

13. William Cronon, "The Trouble with Wilderness," in William Cronon, ed., *Uncommon Ground: Toward Reinventing Nature* (New York: W. W. Norton and Co., 1995), 85–86.

14. Sigurd F. Olson, "The Spiritual Aspects of Wilderness," in David

Brower, ed., *Wilderness: America's Living Heritage* (San Francisco: Sierra Club, 1961), 25.

15. Sigurd F. Olson, *Listening Point* (New York: Alfred A. Knopf, 1958), 153.

16. Olson, *Runes,* 14; Sigurd F. Olson, *Reflections from the North Country* (New York: Alfred A. Knopf, 1976), 88.

17. Olson, *Reflections,* 49.

18. Sigurd Olson, "Reflections of a Guide," *Field and Stream,* June 1928.

19. Olson, "Spiritual Need," 218, 215; Olson, *Reflections,* 35.

20. A good collection of this research is in Jerome H. Barkow, Leda Cosmides, and John Tooby, eds., *The Adapted Mind: Evolutionary Psychology and the Generation of Culture* (New York: Oxford University Press, 1992). Scholars coming from different backgrounds tend to use different labels for similar work. Other common labels include human ecology and sociobiology. One of the field's pioneers was Paul Shepard. See, for example, his book *Coming Home to the Pleistocene* (Washington, D.C.: Island Press, 1998).

21. The note is not dated, but the context places it in August 1960.

The Meaning
of Wilderness

Reflections of a Guide

In the summer of 1923, just a few months after Sigurd Olson and his wife, Elizabeth, moved to Ely, Minnesota, Sigurd found a seasonal job as a guide for Wilderness Outfitters. A biology teacher at Ely's high school, he had been on the payroll only since February, and he needed an income to get through the summer and to save some money in preparation for the baby he and Elizabeth were expecting in September.

Sigurd's experiences during the 1920s as a guide in the Quetico-Superior canoe country of northern Minnesota and Ontario were essential to the development of his wilderness philosophy. Paddling more than a thousand miles every summer, he grew intimately familiar with several million acres of rugged and hauntingly beautiful wilderness. It was as a guide that he began to experience and then to seek the emotionally and spiritually powerful moments of communion that he would later describe as "flashes of insight." But Sigurd's work as a guide added another dimension to his deeply personal encounters with the wild: he got to observe the other guides, and witnessed time and again the reactions of his customers from cities throughout the Midwest. He came to believe that all *people want contact with the wild, and that in the wilderness all but the most hardened eventually shed the false personas of their everyday lives and expose their true selves. As Sigurd developed his voice as a writer and wilderness philosopher, he labeled this instinctive*

reaction to nature "racial memory." (The concept is described in de-
tail in the introduction.)

He did not use that term in "Reflections of a Guide," but this
article—his third published magazine article and second in Field
and Stream—*was his first to apply the basic concept and to exam-*
ine at some length the natural reactions of people when they spend
time in the wild. His conclusions are not entirely romantic. To the
twenty-nine-year-old teacher, guide, and budding writer, it is not
only the silence, solitude, and beauty of wilderness that lifts the spirits
of the average traveler, but also the often grueling work of paddling
and portaging. Indeed, he indicates that the latter is a prerequisite
for fully appreciating the former: it is after a long, physically de-
manding day, when wilderness travelers are fed and resting, that
they most fully appreciate the beauty of the wild and are most
open to experiencing a sense of connectedness to the natural world
around them. And yet Sigurd is realistic enough in this article to
say that the wilderness experience also depends on one's attitude:
"A man's point of view determines whether or not waves are 'white-
capped billows rolling in the sun' or just so much damned water to
be paddled through."

One more observation: Sigurd clearly approves of wilderness
travelers dressing and acting like the fur-trading voyageurs or other
characters from the presettlement past. He does not come right out
and say it yet, but later he will make the point that part of the
wilderness experience is connecting with the human history *of*
the area. This means that learning *about that history is impor-*
tant, and perhaps a bit of role-playing, too, even if it is nothing
more than singing a stanza or two of "En Roulant Ma Boule."

❄ ❄ ❄

GUIDES HAVE BEEN CLASSIFIED, pawed over, and discussed so thoroughly that readers of modern fiction have cause
to feel reasonably well acquainted with them. As a breed, they
are blessed of men, for they live a life more appealing to them
than any other occupation on the face of the earth.

The hermit-like existence they are commonly supposed to enjoy is largely imaginative. True, they do live alone for long periods; but then again, they meet and mingle for months at a time with a variety of people of every class and calling that would be the envy of any social aspirant. In the woods, the bars of social position are let down, and your poor lonesome guide becomes a brother to lawyers, professors, millionaires, and royalty. Fortunate is he who can count among his friends and acquaintances so diversified a list. No wonder, then, that by the time a guide has spent a lifetime living in the close association with people that camp life makes inevitable, he becomes a fair judge of human nature in the raw.

However, it has always been the viewpoint of the man being guided that has been aired. How the guide sees his party and their reactions to camp life is a subject sadly neglected.

In the cities, where discomforts and the ordinary physical struggle for existence have been reduced to the minimum, a man can cover up his normal feelings so well that even the most intimate of his friends know him not. Up in the brush, however, a hundred times a day a man has reason to open up and show what he is really like. Whatever he has been holding in leash will crop out then, be it good or bad.

The longer he lives away from civilization the more natural he becomes. Gone is the smooth veneer that makes him acceptable in society, and he is at last an individual with the God-given right to exercise his own free will. He realizes that civilization has cramped his spirit too long in its effort to mold and make him live his life like millions of other human machines, with no outlet for his pent-up nature.

His new-found personality is often a revelation to him, and he revels in his freedom. Life opens up in a thousand different ways, and every hour spent in the wilderness is packed to the brim with the joyous fulfillment of long dormant desires.

We all have a pronounced streak of the primitive set deep within us, an instinctive longing that compels us to leave the confines of civilization and bury ourselves periodically in the most inaccessible spots we can penetrate. Here we gulp huge lungfuls of sun-washed air, lie on our bellies and drink from rivers and lakes, work, sweat, curse, and sing with the sheer joy of being alive. And what makes guiding the sport of kings is just that. No two men react alike. There is always variety in human nature.

Tenderfoot or old-timer, it makes little difference, for both come into the wild for the same purpose. To the guide, both are adventures in friendship. From the man who has roughed it before he often learns secrets of the woods and waters that he has perhaps been blind to all of his life, and it is always a joy to initiate the tenderfoot into the countless mysteries of the out-of-doors. Both types are a pleasurable experience, and little does the average man know the value his guide places on his friendship.

The man who has lived long in the open is content to drink it in calmly and enjoy himself in the mellow light of life-long experience and understanding. His is the serene enjoyment of the man who has weighed his values and retained only those worth while. He is through with experimenting and knows that in his kinship with the wild he is deriving all those things that to him make living complete.

On the other hand, the man who is new cannot get his fill of violent gratification. The long hours of bending to the paddle, oftentimes in the teeth of a gale, and the heart-wrenching work on swampy portages and steep rocky trails are more than compensated for by the feeling that for once he is really alive and living as a man should live. To him there is no joy quite so complete, or content quite so blissful, as that which comes at the end of a killing portage, when he can flop down to rest, half dead of exhaustion.

He feels then, more than at any other time, that the void created by too much city life is gradually being filled up. Worry is a thing of the past, and all that matters is the glorious present. At night, after a long day of cruising through lakes, running

rapids, and making portages, his bodily wants satisfied, with
nothing ahead but rest and peace under the stars, the full realization comes to him, and then he understands why men go
into the wilderness.

Whether he is a woodsman or not, the average man likes at
least to act like one and give to his guide and the members of
his party that "been there feeling." When the last outposts of
civilization have faded away, your city man begins to shed his
air of reserve and adopts instead the sangfroid of the Canadian
voyageur. He sings songs he hasn't sung since boyhood and
college days, tells stories and laughs uproariously at his own
jokes, smokes and curses to his heart's content, and feels like
the toughest sourdough in the north.

When the waves are rolling high, he grits his teeth and plows
into them fearlessly. What does it matter if water is being shipped and the waves are piling high? Today he's an adventurer in
the land of romance, ready to die with his boots on.

At the portages he singles out the heaviest packs, buckles
down like a Hudson Bay packer, and delights in showing up
his guide. No matter if he is half dead at the end, he can glory
in his strength and bay his prowess at the moon. A guide can't
help but have a warm spot in his heart for men of that caliber,
and he can't help but feel that most men are brothers under
their skins when once they come down to earth.

The same spirit that makes a man want to act like a woodsman
when he is up in the big sticks makes him also want to look like
one. If he is imaginative at all, the more he looks like Daniel
Boone or Davy Crockett the more he enjoys himself. I don't
mean that men go to any extremes in the matter of dress, but
most of them affect some article or other that for some reason
appeals strongly to them.

When a man is trying to live another life entirely, he naturally wants to appear as romantic as his conscience will let him.
It may be an old checkered shirt or battered hat. Whatever it
is, it is usually something in which he thinks he looks or feels

particularly well. If it has once become part and parcel of his outdoors life, he will wear it till it falls apart, rather than get a more serviceable garment.

I have an old army hat that I should have thrown away years ago. It is as full of holes and as disreputable as any old hat can be that has knocked around the woods for over a decade. Yet if I sally forth without it, there is a feeling of loss and incompleteness. I will probably have to wear it another ten years before I have the heart to discard it.

Of all the examples of masculine vanity, an old red shirt worn by my friend Donald Hough occupies the most prominent place in my memory. Years ago, when Don was still cruising for the Forest Service, the old red homespun was a familiar landmark in the border country. It was even then long past its prime.

Several years after, on a trip we took together, the old relic was still very much in evidence, though sadly faded and patched together. At the end of this cruise, I thought it was high time, if Don was to preserve his self-esteem, that some one take the matter in hand. Knowing it would be a delicate proceeding at best, I postponed it till the time came to say goodbye.

I felt that, as a result of my interference in a matter as vital to any man as doing away with an old shirt, our friendship might hang in the balance. Nevertheless I solemnly pleaded with him to put it quietly out of the way and give it a decent interment. He promised faithfully to do what he could, and I left him, assured that I had gazed on the old red homespun for the very last time.

A year later, when in from a trip, what should I see but a familiar splotch of red come wandering down the street. Sure as life, it was Don Hough setting out on a snow-shoe trip through the Superior National Forest. He saw me at about the same time I saw him and approached warily. At about ten paces we both stopped. The moment was tense.

"Don," I said slowly, "can you explain why that thing is up here again?"

For a moment he said nothing, but our eyes met, and in that instant the great realization came to me—"It was the love that passeth all understanding." I promised Don then that as far as I was concerned, he could wear it until it rotted on his back. So the chances are that it is still doing valiant service and will for many a year to come.

Though the men who come into the Canadian border country react as a rule much the same to camp life, nevertheless they vary so widely that a rough classification would not be amiss. The guides group them usually as fishermen, long-distance record-breakers, and true woodsmen. Of course, all three are fishermen, but when I classified one type as purely fishermen, I had in mind those who come up for the fishing alone.

This type is perhaps the hardest problem for the guide. When the fish are not striking, the cruise is a failure; and when they are, it soon becomes monotonous. After about three days of wonderful fishing, the excitement of pulling out more fish than the camp has any use for palls, and discontentment prevails. In vain are the beauties of the scenery extolled, but nothing can satisfy. The fishing for fishing's sake alone soon becomes mechanical; and no matter how ideal other conditions may be, the fisherman leaves dissatisfied.

The long-distance record-breaker is the busiest man of the season. To him the cruise means a wonderful chance for a workout and nothing else. Going from dawn till dusk, he stops for nothing. He fishes for meat, not for sport, and travels through beautiful lakes at breakneck speed.

I well remember a doctor from Missouri, a record-breaker of the first degree. We had been out two weeks and had covered a stretch of country in that time that usually took a month of steady traveling. Our route one day led within a mile of Curtain Falls, one of the most wonderful spots in the border country. Parties traveled great distances to reach it and often camped near for days to take pictures and satisfy their craving for natural beauty. From where we were we could hear distinctly the roar

of falling water. It was growing dark; and as we had cruised
since dawn, I suggested that we go the half mile out of our
way, view the falls, and perhaps camp there.

Not stopping to take his paddle out of the water, the doctor
answered hurriedly: "Don't think we'd better. Got to keep on
paddling if we're going to make our thirty miles."

I knew there was no decent camp site within ten miles or so,
but said nothing and dug in my paddle. It grew steadily darker,
but instead of looking for a landing I kept right on as though
we had all the time in the world. About 8:30 the doctor turned
around and asked wonderingly, "Well, aren't we going to pitch
camp and eat pretty soon?"

Without missing a stroke I answered: "I'm not hungry yet.
Let's make her thirty-five before we quit."

He said nothing, but kept on paddling. We finally did land
about 10:30 P.M., made a miserable camp in the dark, and ate
a cold cheerless supper of cheese and hardtack. At the end of
three weeks we had made a wonderful record of distance covered, but we had missed all of the beauty and restful peace that can
only come when one takes time to let the wilderness soak in.

The man who gets the utmost in enjoyment out of his cruise
is never in a hurry or too busy. He never has a goal he must reach
at a certain time. Beauty he sees in everything and knows that to
do anything merely for its own sake is a waste of time. He never
keeps on fishing until he is tired of it and never keeps more than
he can use. If the fish are not biting, he takes the fact for granted,
does not blame the guide or the country, and proceeds to enjoy
himself in other ways.

He swears by the seven gods that the scenery is the most wonderful he has ever seen. Though the guide is not responsible,
as a good many seem to think, he nevertheless feels an inborn
pride in the country and a sense of ownership that makes him
extremely sensitive about it. A man who makes depreciatory re-
marks and comes with the attitude of "Is this all there is to see?"
will never get next to the inner workings of his guide and never
learn the countless secrets of wild life and wilderness legend
that are woven in with the character of every country.

Contrary to popular opinion, scenery hunting is perhaps the most fickle of enjoyments. To the man steeped in wilderness life, it is always enjoyable; but to those whose sensibilities and values are still governed by their physical natures, it is a variable entity. Plainly speaking, in order to be appreciated, scenery must be viewed against a background of physical comfort and mental relaxation.

Under ideal conditions, I have seen tourists entranced at the beauty of a heavily timbered rock point jutting out into a wilderness lake. Again, I have seen them curse roundly at the same point and at the waves breaking over it. A man's point of view determines whether or not waves are "white-capped billows rolling in the sun" or just so much damned water to be paddled through.

The most beautiful scenery is always seen after a meal. Then, more than at any other time, is a man at peace with the world and most receptive to all its wonders. This truth was brought strikingly home to me on a trip taken two years ago. It was late afternoon and we were up against it for a camp site. We had bucked the wind since morning on Big Saganaga, hoping to camp that night in Seagull Lake.

Try as we might, dusk found us working up the Seagull River, still a long way from our goal. Hungry and tired, we were in no mood to admire scenery, so paddled on in grim silence, searching the steep, inhospitable shores for a landing. Finally we heard the roar of a rapids around a bend in the river and realized, with sinking hearts, that another portage was ahead. Not a man in the party wanted to make that portage, and each one knew it.

We landed at the foot of the rapids, unloaded without a word and started to pitch camp on one of the steepest, rockiest slopes we had seen. Somehow camp was made and supper gotten under way in spite of the unpromising character of the camp site.

After the meal, which was one of those rare affairs when everything happens to be just right, one by one, under the additional influence of good tobacco and dry moccasins, we began to notice what a truly marvelous spot we had stumbled into. The rapids tumbled down through a rocky gorge into a broad, placid pool below our camp. Tall spruces lined the shore, and where the rock was too steeply sloping for trees to secure a foothold it was covered by a carpet of varicolored mosses and lichen.

Gone was the weariness, gone the memories of portaging and miles of paddling; nothing was left but a feeling of lazy contentment. We all sat smoking and drinking it in for what seemed like a long while. Finally Bill, who had cussed at the camp site more than any one else, broke the silence. He had been sitting on a rock overlooking the river, watching the long streaks of foam float down from the rapids. When he spoke, it was from the bottom of his heart.

"Boys," he said slowly and with conviction, "this is one of the most beautiful places we have ever been in."

We all silently agreed with him, for it was as nearly perfect as anything could be. The wisdom of the old saying came back to me then more strongly than ever before, that "The source of all contentment comes from within."

To the true woodsman, the wilderness is always at its best. Of course, his appreciation of its beauties is tempered by his own physical well-being; but no matter what the weather or how adverse the conditions, he always enjoys it. The simple things give him the greatest pleasure—colors, sounds, smells, and the countless other things that go to make life in the wild packed to the brim with the fulfillment of cherished longings.

He believes and adopts whole-heartedly the motto of the guides in the canoe country, that "No matter how wet and cold you are, you're always warm and dry." He applies this versatile philosophy to all situations and as a result is the most happy-go-lucky, care-free mortal in existence. Nothing phases him, and his resultant state of mind is one of rare receptiveness to the beauties and joys of life in the woods.

When in the wilderness, all else is forgotten. He does not count as wasted any time spent watching the clouds, the trees, or the waters. To him, those hours are precious, for it is then that he is storing up a wealth of memories that will help him tide over the times when the stress of city life bears too heavily upon him, and make him forget the struggle in a vision of clear blue skies and sunlit woods and waters.

Field and Stream, June 1928

Search for the Wild

Sigurd was especially fond of this article throughout his life because it was his first published piece devoted entirely to the meaning of wilderness. At the time, however, he must have felt at least a twinge of disappointment, because Sports Afield *made the bizarre editorial decision to split his rather short article into two pieces, publishing the first ten paragraphs in May and the final seven in June. Even so, in an era when the mantra of outdoor magazine editors was "action, action, action!" Sigurd was fortunate to get this published at all. His friendship with Robert C. Mueller, managing editor at* Sports Afield, *may well have made the difference. They became friends in the late 1920s when Sigurd guided Mueller on a canoe trip through the Quetico-Superior wilderness. Mueller took an interest in Sigurd's writing career, and in 1929 he began publishing Sigurd's articles. Most of them were action-filled, light-hearted hunting and fishing stories; four of them were quite poor pieces of north-woods fiction that, Sigurd confessed decades later in* Open Horizons, *probably saw the light of day only because of Mueller's friendship. But Sigurd was good enough and apparently popular enough to get thirteen articles published in* Sports Afield *during the 1930s, a decade in which the magazine's circulation grew from seventy thousand to more than two hundred and fifty thousand. Mueller later credited Sigurd's writing as playing an important role in the magazine's growth.*

This article continues to address the concept of "racial memory"; perhaps most interesting is Sigurd's statement that love of a simple life connected to nature "is still deeply rooted and it will be hundreds or thousands of years before we lose very much of it." This implies something that Sigurd would explicitly state to Bob Marshall six years later, that he believed this attachment to nature had a biological origin. If so, there exists the possibility of gradually losing the attachment in the future, as evolution continues to shape the development of the human species.

"Search for the Wild" also marks Sigurd's first attempt to describe what he would come to call "intangible values" (he says "intangible something" here)—those aspects of the wilderness experience that are impossible to measure or to put a dollar value on, but that are closest to the heart of the average wilderness traveler, such as watching the sun set and the moon rise, tasting fresh-caught walleyed pike or a handful of blueberries, or listening to the cry of a loon at dusk.

When the article came out, Sigurd was searching for the wild in his own way: he was finishing his University of Illinois master's thesis on the timber wolf, hating every minute of it, and writing in his journal that he could not wait to leave Champaign-Urbana and return to the waterways of his beloved canoe country. By the time the second part of the article came out in June, Sigurd was home.

✳︎ ✳︎ ✳︎

THOSE WHO GO FORTH INTO WILD, unsettled regions, if asked the reason for their travels will give a variety of answers. For some it will be fishing, others hunting and the securing of trophies, still others to photograph, explore, or conduct scientific investigations. Most men believe that they "go in" for some definite, concrete purpose. If they are made to admit the true motive behind their wilderness journeys they will, with few far-flung exceptions, agree that it is something entirely different, a purpose for which the very evident ulterior motive is only an excuse.

It is very true that when a man goes into the woods to fish,

he in all probability heads for the lakes and streams; if it is
ducks, the rice beds and marshes know him well. Whatever
it is and wherever it takes him is really immaterial when compared to the underlying reason. What he is really looking for
is that intangible something he calls "the Wild," and if he hunts
or fishes hard enough, he will find it in the close contact with
nature those pursuits entail. Thoreau expresses what most of
us feel in Walden Pond.

> We need the tonic of wildness, to wade sometimes in marshes
> where the bittern and the meadow hen lurk, and hear the
> booming of the snipe, to smell the whispering sedge where
> only some wilder and more solitary wildfowl builds her nest,
> and the mink crawls with its belly close to the ground. At the
> same time that we are earnest to explore and learn all things,
> we require that all things be mysterious and unexplorable, that
> land and sea be infinitely wild, unsurveyed and unfathomed
> by us because unfathomable. We can never have enough of
> Nature. We must be refreshed by the sight of inexhaustible
> vigour, vast and titanic features, the seacoast with its wrecks,
> the wilderness with its living and decaying trees, the thunder
> cloud and the rain which lasts three weeks and produces
> freshets. We need to witness our own limits transgressed and
> some life pasturing freely where we never wander.

So spoke Thoreau, the naturalist and philosopher. To him the
wilderness was a spring at which he continually refreshed himself and renewed his strength. John Burroughs speaking of him
said, "He went to nature as to an oracle and though indeed
very often questioned her as a naturalist and a poet, yet there
was always another question in his mind. He ransacked the
country about Concord, in all seasons and in all weathers, and
all times of the day and night, he delved into the ground, he
probed the swamps, he searched the waters, he dug into wood-
chuck holes, into muskrat dens, into the retreats of mice and
squirrels, he saw every bird, heard every sound, found every wild
flower, and brought home many a fresh bit of natural history;
but he was always searching for something he did not find."

I do not agree with Burroughs' last sentence, for I am confident that the lifelong search of Thoreau was not entirely unfruitful. What he sought in his daily rambles through the woods and fields surrounding Concord and Walden Pond, is what we all seek when we go into the wilds. Sometimes we are successful and sometimes we are not, but we never come back without having found some slight vestige at least of that for which we sought. It is the underlying motive for trips and expeditions, this constant, neverending search for the wild, and it is compensation enough for all discomforts, trials, and tribulations encountered enroute.

Those who have been much in the field have also learned long ago that although it is extremely pleasant to come back with the limit of birds or trout, still the day is not spoiled if there was only one or two or even none. The fact that during a day in the open a man may have absorbed some of the very essence of the out-of-doors, itself, is then considered ample payment and no day in the wild is ever wasted.

To most men the wild and contact with it are a necessary part of existence. To some it means more than to others, all depending upon the potency of their primitive inheritance. Some are satisfied with a week or two out of the year; others must "go in" for months at a time. Many would go in more often than that if they only could. No matter what the classification to which you belong, the craving is there to a greater or lesser degree and must be satisfied, and more it is something which cannot be put off lightly or postponed. The penalty for disregard is too severe and self denial when the call is strong results inevitably in frayed nerves, loss of enthusiasm and appetite for present modes of existence. The urge to escape the rush and unnaturalness of urban life and make intimate and forceful contact with the earth once more is a more powerful incentive than most men care to admit even to themselves.

After all it is little wonder, when we consider that we are not far removed as yet from the day of the early pioneer and woodsman, not so far removed that the old ties may be severed with impunity.

A half century ago, much of this country was still wild and un-settled. Many of us spent our boyhood days on wilderness farms or ranches, in the neighborhood of lumber camps or isolated frontier communities. If we did not, it is safe to assume that our parents or grandparents did. It is a long jump from the life of those days to the concentrated civilization of our cities and larger towns and it is rather hopeless to believe that in the short space of a generation or two, we can completely root out of our systems the love of the simple life and the primitive. It is still deeply rooted and it will be hundreds or thousands of years before we lose very much of it. It is an inheritance so deeply in-grained in our natures that it can never be stifled. We are still adventurers of the wilderness and must answer the call in order to keep our equilibrium. Once we lose our touch with the wild and we lose our perspective, too long a time on the pavements and we starve for the smell and touch of virile earth.

It was this that Thoreau meant when he said, "We need the tonic of the wild." Inasmuch as our natures are still rooted firm-ly in the soil, we need to renew frequently our contact with the simplicity of life in the out-of-doors. Those who need artificial stimulation, crowds, and creature comforts without the neces-sity of working for them, have no place in the wilderness. Only those who can live frugally and simply can be really happy in the wild. They, on the other hand, who feel that they have been robbed of their inheritance by having had everything done for them, accept with joy the challenge of doing for themselves.

After all, what a man craves most is the old struggle for the bare necessities of existence, food, warmth, and shelter, not to mention the stimulus and alertness due to constant battle with natural enemies. City life deprives a man of all that, and makes of the physical side of life so secure and easy a thing, that he re-volts at the protection offered him.

Living happily in the out-of-doors means getting down to the bare essentials. The man who goes in with all of the claptrap necessary to give him a semi-civilized existence in the wilderness is defeating at once the very purpose for which he went in. The mark of a real woodsman is one who can live comfortably in the wilderness with the least expenditure of energy, but that in the last analysis means living simply and with economy. If your wants are few and limited to only those things which are absolutely necessary for reasonable animal comfort, your life in the wild cannot help but be successful and happy. If, on the other hand, you are not attuned to the spirit of the out-of-doors and still feel the need of luxury and pampering, you have lost at the very beginning what you really came into the wild to find.

By renewing his contact with natural things a man recreates himself, by performing natural primitive tasks, by seeing and feeling things of the earth he is strengthened. That is why we get such keen and wholesome pleasure from simple tasks on the trail or in camp. We enjoy doing the primitive things we so long have been denied. Our muscles long for action and thrill at the performance of duties long forgotten. Then, too, there is a mental satisfaction which only comes from doing things with our hands and we delight in developing once again a skill with tool or weapon.

We all admit the marvelous convenience of municipal heat in town, nevertheless, we crave the sensation of direct contact with the flame. When we cut our own wood, we impart to it some of our own energy and when we warm our hands before the flame, it seems doubly good to us, because we were directly instrumental in bringing it about. We sit watching the coals at night, entranced by the mystery of their glow, watch the smoke curl up and disappear in the tree tops with an inward satisfaction we never knew in town.

How good and sweet water can taste that has been carried from a spring a quarter of a mile away over a dark and treacherous trail. How we husband every precious drop, measuring it out carefully as though it were a high priced beverage, which in truth it is. How good to lie on the ground and drink from a gurgling riffle in some tiny stream. As we drink, we watch the

shifting of the sand and gravel on the bottom and see the wav-
ing of the water plants and mosses in the current. The act of
drinking itself becomes a pleasure and not merely a means
of laving our thirst. A little more of a dip and the ripple flows
over your face, a most delightful and legitimate sensation, but
how ridiculous and criminal a performance at a public drinking fountain in town.

What a joy it is to pitch a tent, our home for a night or as
long as we please. The very uncertainty and the possibility of
choice amid new and strange surroundings makes it a pleasure
in itself, a real adventure at the close of the day. First we exam-
ine this spot and then that, finally deciding on a point that not
only is smooth and level but will give us air and view. The way
the tent should face is a most important question and we weigh
the factors concerned with solemnity. If it faces this way, we
shall miss the morning sun and will sleep late; that way, we shall
rise with the dawn and besides have a timbered island cruising
before us. That decided, the tent smells soon again of balsam
boughs. Everything is ready for the night and nothing to do but
listen to the sounds of the night birds, talk over the adventures
of the day, and rest.

And what a delightful sensation it is to relax and stretch
weary muscles after a day of wilderness travel. In order to really
appreciate rest we must first experience fatigue and without experiencing fatigue we cannot ever hope to know the complete
mental relaxation that comes from muscular effort. That perhaps, more than anything, attunes a man to the wild and not
until he can forget himself, his worries, and the outside does
he fit into the scheme of things in the wilderness.

These are only a few of the things we go into the wilderness for,
the doing of which satisfies to some extent our craving for contact with the earth. There are countless other things that give
us equal pleasure, dawns and sunsets, clouds, the color of leaves,
the finding of a rare flower, watching a beaver build his house,

listening to the whistle of wings over a marsh, not to forget the warble of birds in the sunlight of early morning, and many others, all an intimate part of life in the wild and part and parcel of what we go in to find.

Sports Afield and Trails of the Northwoods, May–June 1932

The Romance of Portages

In 1933, as part of his New Deal program to combat the Great Depression, President Franklin D. Roosevelt created the Civilian Conservation Corps. Over the course of the next nine years the CCC gave much-needed work to two million men. Assigned to the nation's public lands, they planted trees, fought fires, constructed campgrounds and shelters and administrative buildings, and built dams and roads. Their work was usually characterized as "improvements" to the nation's parks and forests, and enjoyed vast public support. While few people questioned the basic goals of the program from an environmental perspective, some argued, however, that not every new road or trail or building was an improvement.

Sigurd Olson was one of the doubters. Even before the creation of the CCC, crews had begun to "improve" old trails and portages in northern Minnesota's canoe country, responding to the tourism boom that began in earnest in the late 1920s as new roads increased access to the region. The CCC hastened the process, and Sigurd watched with growing dismay as log bridges were laid over wilderness creeks and low spots along portages, as trees were trimmed and brush cleared, and as narrow paths were widened, straightened, and graded. In 1936, shortly after becoming dean of Ely Junior College, the thirty-seven-year-old conservationist felt compelled to respond. "The Romance of Portages" was Sigurd's first sustained treatment of the idea that human history *is an essential part of the wilderness experience and adds a unique character to the beauty of a land.*

❄ ❄ ❄

*P*ORTAGE IN THE ORIGINAL FRENCH means a carry between two lakes or rivers, a place of labor in the transportation of supplies and equipment, a break in the monotony of paddling, and perhaps a meeting ground for voyageurs. To all of those who have travelled the wilderness lake country of our own north, it means all of that and more: to those who know the story of the past, portages spell romance. In a country whose hinterlands are difficult of access, where the building of roads and highways borders on the verge of the impossible, rivers and lakes and the portages in between them become the lanes of travel.

For thousands of years, these trails between the waterways have been in use. First by the Indian tribes, the Ojibwa and the Chippewa, and later when the great fur companies began to urge the opening up and exploration of the northwest, by the courier du bois and voyageur. Over the more traveled routes, these ancient trails have been worn deep by moccasined feet, as plainly in evidence today as when they were the only highways of the wilderness. Some of them, however, connecting waters off the regular routes are now dim and almost forgotten, covered with the moss and lichen and duff of an obliterating vegetation.

To the canoe traveler, portages may be a source of pleasure or just an unwelcome chore. Always they are a break in the routine of paddling and a rest for the eyes that are weary with long distances and the glare of sunlight on the water, but to those who love them most and understand, they speak of human associations from the past, of other voyageurs who have gone before. Sometime long ago, before our continent was ever dreamed of by the wandering tribes of Europe, some Indian hunters first bruised that carpet of caribou moss and blazed the trail for the many who would follow. Here on this gravelly beach, stealthy war parties unloaded their canoes and watchful of the enemy crossed perhaps in the dark of night. Many a battle was fought on such connecting trails and many a tale of ambush and bloody conflict could they tell.

Here came the great loads of the fur brigades, two ninety-pound packets of fur or equipment per man and more if he were strong. Picturesque wilderness men were those early French from old Quebec and Montreal, sons of adventure and exploration. Here are the same landing rocks on which they unloaded their burdens, here the same riffles and currents which they had to fight in order to beach safely their fragile canoes, here the same vistas and in some places even the trees. We know they traveled the waters, but lakes and rivers always change and lose association with the past. It is different with portages for here man is close to the earth and leaves indelible evidence of his passing.

Portages like other things with which we are familiar develop personality as we endow them with human associations and past experience. Things that have been long lived with, that have known joy and sorrow, failure and success, work and rest, these things we think of differently. They have become a part of the human picture, part and parcel of our lives and we feel toward them as we can only feel toward things which we know well. All old trails and roads have their allure and we follow them easily, knowing that many have gone before. New roads, garish and raw, though they may serve us well and fill a place, are never the same as the old for they lack the touch of having been lived with and used and have to serve their apprenticeship in the life of a race before they become an intimate part and expression of personality.

No two portages are alike, each has a character and definite personality of its own, developed partly through our own individual associations with it and partly through its past history. Only a few portages have names and only those which have played a significant part in the lives of wilderness travelers. Such a one is the Portage of Singing Creek, connecting the waters of Burke and Sunday Lake just north of the international border. Someone long ago called it Singing Creek and the name fits it well, for the little brook which flows beside it has a musical trickle all its own. Here too is a camp where many a party has stopped after battling the waves of Sunday or the long pull down the twenty-mile sweep of Agnes to the west and here, to the soothing sound of flowing water, they have rested and slept.

To any of those who have traveled the Kawishowa River in the Superior Forest, the Snowbank Portage will bring memories, but to those who live nearby, it brings visions of first trips after the spring breakup, the joy of wet and soggy earth, oozy muskeg, and the pungent odor of swelling buds. And who can forget after the long two miles of rocky ridge and swamp and beaver flow, the first sight of the broad blue sheet of Snowbank Lake sparkling in the spring sunshine and the trout that were always there?

Then there is the portage round Pipestone Falls into Basswood Lake, the entrance to the wilderness. Here parties fresh from the towns and cities leave civilization and head for the border and new adventures. Here they see the wild for the first time and know the unforgettable sensation of leaving everything behind and at last being entirely on their own. No matter if they never return again, that first thrilling glimpse of the unknown burns itself into their memories.

One of the most famous portages in the north is "Grand Portage" around the falls and rapids of the Pigeon River near Lake Superior, nine miles of tortuous rugged trail. At its very foot is now the little town of Grand Portage where in the old days landed the flotillas and brigades of fur canoes from Quebec and Montreal. At the upper end is the site of Fort Charlotte, long headquarters of the Northwest Fur Company. Here at one time lived hundreds of men and over this trail came the bulk of the fur from the great Northwest. Grand Portage then was a name to conjure with in the annals of exploration and development of our north. Now it is no longer a traveled wilderness road and the years have all but hidden it from view. To those who know however and can read the language of the bush, there still is abundant evidence of the days when its fame was known from coast to coast.

And there are many others, Dieu Riviere up in the country of Pickerel Lake, Battle Portage up toward Lac La Croix, Prairie Portage, gateway to the east, Dead Man's Portage, the far famed Kashapiwi, and countless others, each with its own particular story of hard, joyous days of wilderness travel. Some of them were known of old and some we have named in our own cruising, but no matter under which category they fall, during the years we learn to love them, each rock and windfall, and muck-bottomed bog. On the portages, we feel at home with the country and it is here we really know the wild.

Portages always followed the easiest and shortest routes and were always chosen after much reconnoitering and climbing of hills. Once, they were blazed and travelled, they did not change, but were worn deeper and deeper by constant use. Natural elevations were always taken into consideration, smooth ledges that were easy on moccasined feet. Like all woods trails, they were always winding, avoiding such natural obstructions as rocks and windfalls or patches of sphagnum. As the years went on, however, they were gradually straightened and today very old portages can always be recognized by the fact that they are as direct as the natural topography would permit. Often they were close enough to the connecting rivers so that one might always see the white water of rapids and hear their roar. Such portages are most often named and spoken of, for even though they might be hard, their cost in labor and weariness was more than compensated for by the sheer poetry of their setting. And hardened though a woodsman may be and loath to admit it, still deep down within his rough exterior is an appreciation of setting and atmosphere that is second to none, and old portages to him are sacred.

Through the lake regions of our state during the past decade, there has been much improvement of portage trails, clearing out of brush, trimming of trees, straightening out of turns, and grading of the old deeply worn ruts. Granted that from a purely practical point of view, such improvement is necessary for those who make a business of wilderness travel, forest rangers and patrol men, game wardens, and others. Looked at from a purely utilitarian angle, we must admit that shortening trails, widening them to the status of fire lanes, building bridges over low spots and creeks, putting in docks at the landing and concrete fireplaces to replace the old smoke blackened hearths of years gone by, is all worthwhile in the name of efficiency, but considered from the standpoint of those who go into the forest for recreation, it is a different matter entirely and a tragic one.

Those who go into the wilderness for their pleasure are philosophers and dreamers and they may travel far for the enjoyment that only the wild can give. They do not come entirely for the fishing or the game or even for scenery, though all these may be important. What they come for most is atmosphere and the feeling that here things have not changed, that here is the charm of the old and primitive. Deprive a country or a portage of its atmosphere by too much artificialization and you have taken from it its personality, for one is empty without the other. Make the old trails all alike, make them merely convenient swiftly travelled roadways between the lakes and the thrill of knowing them is gone. One might as well try and improve an old masterpiece mellowed by age as try and improve a portage that has been used for centuries. The result is the same, a sacrifice of inherent uniqueness for the efficiency of the new.

The canoe country of the Superior-Quetico region is as different from the rest of the continent as the Rockies themselves differ from the plains and foothills which approach them. Here is a wilderness lake country which for sheer beauty and unique topographical structure has no equal anywhere. We have passed laws preserving the shorelines from despoliation and it is time we passed other laws to save those portions of the ancient water lanes that connect them, the portages, and do nothing to improve or alter them beyond keeping them in the shape they would have been kept in by ordinary wilderness travel. In certain of the more settled parts of the lake country improvement of an artificial nature may be necessary, but in those regions which today have a distinctly wilderness aspect and as such have aesthetic values far more important than the purely practical, the program of portage improvement should be weighed very carefully.

What is needed is a new conception and appreciation of the meaning of portages. If we look at them in the light of old associations and as monuments to the days of the past, we see more than a carry between two lakes, a place of work or rest. We see them as the ancient wilderness roads of a race, relics of an adventurous past, rarities which in our time are becoming exceedingly precious. Seen through the eyes of people who know these things and understand the intangible values of atmosphere, improvement for entirely practical reasons is unwarranted.

These portage trails of ours are part and parcel of a priceless spiritual heritage, the old wilderness. Being part of it, we cannot possibly hope to retain one without the other. Wilderness is a delicate adjustment, one which can be disarranged very quickly and when in addition to its original primitive value, it has bound up irretrievably with it a romantic human history, then it becomes doubly imperative that the utmost care be taken in its administration for fear of disturbing values which can never be replaced.

Minnesota Conservationist, April 1936

Let's Go Exploring

In "The Wilderness World of Sigurd F. Olson," filmed near the end of Sigurd's life, there is a scene in which Elizabeth Olson reads aloud a portion of an essay Sigurd was working on: "The search for the spot of blue, no matter what it means to the individual, is always worthwhile." Sigurd, listening to her, responds, "And don't you think that this is a common quest? Everyone's looking for a spot of blue; without that spot of blue you don't know where to go, you have no direction in your life."

To Sigurd, "the search for the spot of blue" was a metaphor that referred to the intellectual quest for knowledge and, even more importantly, to the spiritual search for meaning. Forty-some years earlier, when he wrote about the "spot of blue" in the following Field and Stream *article, he did not elevate the phrase to the level of metaphor. The article as whole, however, captures part of the meaning he later gave to the metaphor—the joy of discovery and of the sometimes difficult journey that leads to discovery. For Sigurd, an ideal wilderness trip is as much an interior journey as it is an exterior one. The prerequisites are space and solitude, and the desire to search for the spot of blue.*

THERE IS ONE THRILL THAT NEVER GROWS OLD—the
thrill of seeing for the first time new land or water. If it happens
to be water and you are a fisherman, then the thrill is doubly
keen. By "new water," I do not mean water that is new to you
only, but new to everyone; a spot of blue that has never been
on a fisherman's map, something untried and untouched.

Who has not dreamed of some day finding just that sort of
paradise and of joining the ranks of the explorers that have gone
before him? What is more discouraging than a map that shows
an intricate maze of highways, specked with countless towns and
cities? Most of us have sometime wished that we had been born
a generation or two ago, when the land beyond the Alleghenies
was wild and unknown.

In spite of the crowded appearance of the ordinary road
map to the would-be explorer, there is still much to be thank-
ful for. Map distances are deceiving, and between some of the
lines and dots are great areas unpenetrated by road or trail—
real wilderness where a man can roam to his heart's content
and satisfy the primitive longing to explore.

One of these areas lies on the Minnesota-Ontario border,
embraced on the south by the Superior National Forest and on
the north by the Quetico Provincial Park of Ontario. Here lie
some ten million acres of primitive canoe country that are wild
and undeveloped. True, the major canoe routes have been well
mapped, for they are the highways of the wilderness, as they
have been for hundreds of years. In between them, however,
are hundreds of unmapped strips which on the map seem to
be mere slivers of space but which are actually miles and miles
across.

Great valleys and hills of aspen and pine cover these areas;
lakes alive with bass, trout, and pike; unknown shores where
moose and deer feed undisturbed and the only sound besides
their splashing is the call of the loon. In this country a man can
hide away for weeks or months and never see another soul,
provided he is an adventurer at heart.

To reach such country may mean backbreaking toil over uncut portages, strange uncharted rapids, uncleared camp sites and a gambling chance at fishing, for not every new water is a fishing El Dorado. The uncharted routes may not be as beautiful as those that are known, but the lure is there, the will-o'-the-wisp which has beckoned to explorers since the beginning of time. When a man has seen country that is new, when once he has known the joy of discovery, he becomes a member of a great world-wide fraternity whose password, spoken in a hundred tongues, means "wilderness."

As a resident of the lake country of the north, I have had abundant opportunity to indulge my own craving and introduce many others to its pleasures. Some come back year after year, never quite satisfied; for others, one taste is enough to stifle the small urge they thought was there.

There is one man who will cruise until the day he dies and who hopes some day to leave his bones on some barren hilltop in the Canadian lake country—old John MacNally. I'll never forget the first time I met Mac, nor the first thing he told me after our frontier introduction.

"I don't care where we go," he said, "or what kind of fishing we get, just as long as you promise to take me somewhere off the map."

I looked at him unbelievingly and could have danced for joy. Although most guides love every trail they travel, the opportunity of working into something new is the kind of trip they always dream of. For three solid months I had made the conventional trips along the well-known border routes, and when Mac's wire came in to the outfitting post I had no idea that this would be anything but just another cruise.

Mac must have sensed immediately the bond between us, for he did not mention route again, content in the knowledge that we were going places. Here was a man I would not have to worry about, a man who knew what he wanted. The trip was already a success, and we went about our packing with all the joyous enthusiasm of a couple of boys out for the first time. When all was ready, the last bit of grub and equipment stowed safely away, paddles tested and the canoe checked, we took one last look at the big map on the warehouse wall and shoved off toward the border.

A week of paddling and portaging down the beautiful western boundary route and a run straight north into the country of Elk Lake brought us to the shores of Bart Lake. We pitched camp that night to the accompaniment of a hundred screaming gulls. To the north of us lay a heavily wooded ridge, and beyond that the unknown.

The next morning, after an early breakfast, we cut back into the brush toward the ridge towering to the north of us. What a day for exploring! The sun was just peeping over the tops of the spruces; dew was heavy on the alders and striped maples; birds were singing, and there was not a cloud in the sky.

At first the going was hard, but as we worked away from the shore the underbrush thinned and gave way to a mixed growth of pine, spruce, and aspen. We finally reached a sheer bluff towering a hundred feet above us and had to detour a quarter of a mile to get around it.

Near the summit of the great ridge the trees became thinner, leaving only a scattering stand of scrub jack-pine, hardy clumps of juniper, and patches of caribou moss. Suddenly we found ourselves on a bare ledge, smooth and glaciated. For the first time since we began our climb we saw Bart far below us, a blue and sparkling gash in the mottled green of the valley we had left. We hadn't realized that we had come so far or had gotten so high above the lake. The summit itself was close, and we could see the rounded slope beyond which was nothing but space.

At last we passed the final fringe of jack-pine, climbed on to the open ledge—and the whole wilderness lay before us. Miles and miles of billowing hills with great valleys in between them; hills dark with spruce and pine, checkered with the lighter hues of aspen and birch—a green undulating carpet unbroken by fire or ax. This was the real wilderness. Here were space and solitude.

Mac was the first to speak. "You know," he said slowly as he filled his pipe, "following these canoe routes is all right; but after all, it's a lot like traveling down a city street hedged in with skyscrapers. All you see is the sky and the walls. Even the portages in this country give one the feeling of crawling through burrows in the brush. You really don't see anything until you get on top, no matter where you are."

And Mac was right, although I had never thought of it in just that way. After all, a canoe traveler cruising down the water lanes, even though he does enjoy the gorgeous panorama of lake-shore points and islands and an occasional sweeping view of distant ridges, does not get the full expanse of the country itself until he leaves the trail and takes to the heights. He never forgets that first sensation of distance. As we gazed at Bart, far below us, just a winding, broken ribbon of blue in a jagged valley, we realized the bigness of the country and its charm.

In the midst of our reflection I recalled what had brought us here—not the view, wonderful as it was, but the search for a spot of blue off the beaten trail, new water for our rods. I jumped to my feet, for in all that great panorama of green there was not a single break. We would have to climb still higher.

"Where to?" asked Mac. "Why don't you settle down and enjoy it while you've got a chance?"

"You haven't forgotten what brought us up here, have you, Mac?" I answered as I headed for a big scraggly jack-pine growing right out over the edge of the cliff.

After I had gotten up about twenty feet, I poked my head through the tangle of branches for my first look. Not a thing but the same rolling ridges. Just as I had given up all hope a tiny glimmer of blue caught my eyes, a spot in the very bottom of the great bowl over a mile away. Then for a moment I lost it in the maze of blue and green; so I closed my eyes to rest them.

When I looked again, the country was freshly new, and there, as I had caught it first, was my spot of blue, now shining steadily. I turned my head this way and that; but when I came back

to the old position, there it was. Here was new water! Had
I been with Balboa when he first saw the blue of the Pacific
or with Boone when he first glimpsed the "dark and bloody
ground" beyond the Alleghenies, I could not have been more
thrilled. This was exploration!

I called loudly to Mac, and he came charging over.

"What's the matter?" he yelled.

I was too busy scrambling higher to answer him. When I
had gone as far as the swaying top would let me, I pushed aside
the impeding branches and swung my glasses into line. We
were in luck, for the little spot of blue proved to be a sizable
body of water, a wilderness lake perhaps a mile in length with
rugged beetling shores and several small islands, one of them
possibly large enough for a camp site. I could plainly see that
the shores were lined with windfalls and some of the bays with
dead birch, the work of beavers, and in one bay there was an
orange spot, a deer without a doubt.

After marking the location carefully with my compass, I
climbed down, gave Mac all the news, then cut once more into
the brush due northwest, down and into the valley. We crossed
several meandering ridges on the way down, and in the very
bottom of the valley waded through a soggy patch of muskeg.

At last we heard the chatter of a kingfisher, and a little later
burst through the alder fringe and found ourselves by water. So
this was our spot of blue! Mac was already down on his knees
sampling it.

"Clear," he sputtered, "clear and cold as Lac La Croix or
Knife. Looks like trout water to me rather than bass, but you
never can tell."

I had pushed my way through to the head of a little bay,
where I could get a good view of the lake. It was at least a mile
in length, with rugged rocky shores capped by rank after rank
of spruce, boggy and rather bassy-looking bays, several beaver
houses, and plenty of dead birch in the shallows. The presence
of beavers, of course, indicated that there was an outlet somewhere, and an outlet meant a connection with some other lake

or stream. There were bass to the south and east; and if that was the direction of flow, then in all probability there would be bass here too.

I waded out to a boulder about twenty feet from shore for a better look at the bottom and to see if there were any minnows about, but not a sign of life did I see. Then a splash toward a small bunch of lily-pads startled me.

"What was that?" asked Mac.

"Don't know," I answered, "but I'll soon find out."

I had picked up a small green frog along the shore for just that purpose, and with a little flip tossed him out toward the pads. He hit with a smack, lay quietly for a moment and then began very slowly to swim for the first big leaf. Had he known that his life was at stake, he wouldn't have moved quite so leisurely; he swam as though this was his own private pool and he was the only frog in it. Just as he placed one hand over the edge of the first lily-pad the water around him boiled, and he disappeared in a circle of spray.

Words were unnecessary. I looked at Mac, and he looked at me.

"Just like a story book," was all he said, but that expressed it beautifully.

We spent the better part of an hour scouting around the shore, sizing things up. Out of the east bay ran a small creek with a beaver dam across it, and in the quiet water just above swam a school of two-pound bass. That was enough; the lake must be alive with them.

The next job was to get the outfit over. Just how we did it we will leave to your imagination. By the afternoon of the following day, however, we were there, with a fair trail blazed from the north end of Bart Lake. It was just before sunset when we shoved our loaded canoe into the water and headed west toward the rocky little island I had seen from the ridge.

Those who have never found new bass water cannot understand the feelings that were ours as we pushed our canoe into the sunset that evening. Here we were, all alone—perhaps the only white men who had ever been on these waters, and surely the only bass fishermen. And to know that here was country entirely primitive was enough to make us more than happy.

The shadows lengthened and the surface of the lake began to take on the hues of sunset; there was no sound but the wild calling of a loon in some lake over the hills and the soft swishing of our paddles. There is something about new country, and a man doesn't have to be a sentimentalist to feel it. It is hard to explain, but the infinite quiet and the sense of strangeness which are always there grow on one, until he is never satisfied unless he has frequent opportunity to indulge his urge for the new.

When we reached the island, we found it grown thickly with spruce and jack-pine, but at one end was an opening covered with caribou moss, all ready for our tent. In our front yard were enough blueberries to last us for a week, and for firewood an old dry pine just ready to topple over—the perfect setup for a wilderness camp.

We landed almost reverently, unloaded the canoe, and surveyed for the first time our little kingdom. From the point of the island we could look over the entire lake—our lake for as long as we wanted to stay. It was the work of only a few moments to string up the tent, build a crude fireplace, and get supper under way.

While we were taking our after-supper smoke a bull moose splashed into a grassy bay not three hundred yards away. That completed the picture, for moose don't stumble into camp sites on the regular routes. This was really off the trail. Mac summed up his feelings in one sentence.

"And to think," he said, "that one short week ago tonight I was down in the Chicago Loop!"

It was the contrast that fascinated Mac as much as anything else. Knowing that both the wilderness and civilization were available to the nth degree, he was completely happy. I have found it is the same with many men; being able to live in the present and also in the past gives them a sense of completeness that they can get in no other way.

There were feeding fish everywhere, and we watched the spreading circles until it grew too dark to see.

The next morning we put our fly rods together and made a few preliminary casts before breakfast. On Mac's second cast he hooked a three-pounder which we cleaned and fried to go with the pancakes. While we were eating breakfast and discussing the day's plans a school of about a dozen, not one under two pounds, swam lazily by. It was hard to believe, but there they were, and we fed them bits of pancake until our supply was gone.

We had decided to explore the lake, but in the face of this performance we could get all the fishing we wanted right from the island. First we tried the flies we knew should work, then anything we happened to have, until we grew weary with pulling them in. By noon, however, they stopped rising, and not a lure we had could coax as much as a nibble.

We did not fish again until late afternoon. Then we paddled down the north shore to fish a few good-looking bays that we could see plainly from the camp site. The game now was for a big one, nothing under five pounds. We were using a barbless bucktail exclusively, as we found they would rise to that favorite northern fly better than for anything else in our books. For half an hour we did nothing. Then, as we slipped around an old abandoned beaver house, Mac got the real strike of the day.

"Hold him!" I yelled. "That's the one we've been waiting for!"

Mac didn't need any cautioning, and handled him beautifully. Backing water, I finally got him out of the tangle of a windfall, but the bass bored right down into the mass of old beaver cuttings below the house. For a moment it looked as though we would lose him. Then, very gently, Mac edged him out into deeper water, and he was safe.

It was now only a matter of patience. Once he came completely out, and danced almost into the canoe. Sunlight and bronze, what a beauty he was! Another five minutes, and he was alongside, fanning his fins slowly.

I slipped the net underneath and lifted him out. Not a big bass by some standards—just 4 pounds 8 ounces—but a clean northern bass, full-bodied and hard, every ounce a fighter, a fish born and bred in clear cold water. We were satisfied, and saved him for supper. Drifting around idly, we caught several more good fish, but none the size of the first.

Both Mac and I had done much bass fishing; but like all dyed-in-the-wool fishermen, we never tired of feeling the flip of the wrist that sets a hook fair and square in the jaw of a scrapper. For a whole week we played around and caught all the bass we wanted to, releasing each one as carefully as though he were the last of the species, keeping only the few we needed for food. Here we had practice in the gentle art of timing a strike just right under all conditions, something that is usually an impossibility in lakes where each strike is an event not to be treated lightly. We learned more real technique from watching each other than we had acquired in many a year.

We didn't name our little lake, and we have never been back. Mac wrote me a short time ago, and I could tell that he was getting the itch to hit the trail once more, not so much to catch bass as to do a little more exploring. Unless I am mistaken, sometime soon I will meet him and we will head for another spot of blue in some forgotten valley of the Quetico.

Field and Stream, June 1937

Why Wilderness?

This was Sigurd's first article about wilderness that was published in a national conservation magazine, but that was not his original intent. Over the course of two years he had sent it to half a dozen prominent magazines, such as the Saturday Evening Post *and* Atlantic Monthly, *and also had entered it in a* Reader's Digest *writing contest, all without success. Still, "Why Wilderness?" was thirty-nine-year-old Sigurd's finest piece of writing thus far, displaying greater confidence and some of the lyrical style for which he would become famous. Wilderness Society founder Bob Marshall, writing to Sigurd on November 12, 1938, called it "as good an article on the wilderness as I have ever read."*

This article was Sigurd's first to use the phrase "racial memory," and Marshall questioned the concept. Sigurd's response on November 22, 1938, indicated not only that he used the term racial *in the inclusive sense of "the human race," but that he believed the primitive attachment to nature he described had a biological origin:*

> *I am confident that a way of life can become deeply implanted in the racial genetic set up. . . . If temperatures, pressures, climatic and nutritional influences may in the long run affect the genes of a species, surely, there should be some background to the idea that a race might actually pass on a deeply rooted feeling for a certain way of life.*

> *I do not believe for an instant that a father can pass on [geneti-*
> *cally] a required skill . . . but I do believe that man as an animal*
> *race has ingrained in his chromosomes a need of freedom, physical*
> *struggle, primitive living, which a few thousand years of living in*
> *towns has not begun to root out. Our genetical research has been*
> *entirely along lines of the physical. Nothing has been done to speak*
> *of along lines of emotion and feeling for things. That is still wilder-*
> *ness as far as geneticists are concerned.*

Bob Marshall, too much a rationalist despite his strong romantic
streak, could not quite accept this fundamental piece of Sigurd's
emerging wilderness doctrine. Nevertheless, as the introduction to
this book explains, in the years since Sigurd's death the basic idea
of racial memory has become the cornerstone of the emerging schol-
arly discipline of evolutionary psychology.

This article, perhaps better than any of his others, describes the
importance of the physical *aspects of the wilderness experience.*
Sigurd maintains that there is a "fierce satisfaction that only comes
with hardship." Fighting the waves, slogging through a mucky
portage with a heavy pack and canoe, setting up camp after a bone-
wearying day, and then sleeping on the ground may not always be
fun, but nevertheless are for many people a stress-releasing break
from a comfortable yet vaguely unsatisfying urban life. The exercise
in itself helps release stress, but in addition is the sense of perspective
that comes from spending days or weeks at a time in which the major
decisions have to do with such basic physical necessities as food and
shelter. Echoing Bob Marshall and Bertrand Russell, Sigurd also ar-
gues that sharing the physical difficulties and the simple pleasures of
a wilderness trip with others can bring about a kind of camaraderie
that otherwise is most often found in the midst of war.

❄ ❄ ❄

IN SOME MEN, THE NEED OF UNBROKEN COUNTRY,
primitive conditions, and intimate contact with the earth is
a deeply rooted cancer gnawing forever at the illusion of con-

tentment with things as they are. For months or years this
hidden longing may go unnoticed and then, without warning,
flare forth in an all consuming passion that will not bear denial.
Perhaps it is the passing of a flock of wild geese in the spring,
perhaps the sound of running water, or the smell of thawing
earth that brings the transformation. Whatever it is, the need
is more than can be borne with fortitude and for the good of
their families and friends, and their own particular restless souls,
they head toward the last frontiers and escape.

I have seen them come to the "jumping off places" of the
North, these men whereof I speak. I have seen the hunger in
their eyes, the torturing hunger for action, distance, and solitude, and a chance to live as they will. I know these men and
the craving that is theirs; I know also that in the world today
there are only two types of experience which can put their
minds at peace, the way of wilderness or the way of war.

As a guide in the primitive lake regions of the Hudson's Bay
watershed, I have lived with men from every walk of life, have
learned to know them more intimately than their closest friends
at home, their dreams, their hopes, their aspirations. I have
seen them come from the cities down below, worried and sick
at heart, and have watched them change under the stimulus
of wilderness living into happy, carefree, joyous men, to whom
the successful taking of a trout or the running of a rapids meant
far more than the rise and fall of stocks and bonds. Ask these
men what it is they have found and it would be difficult for
them to say. This they do know, that hidden back there in the
country beyond the steel and the traffic of towns is something
real, something as definite as life itself, that for some reason or
other is an answer and a challenge to civilization.

At first, I accepted the change that was wrought with the
matter of factness of any woodsman, but as the years went by
I began to marvel at the infallibility of the wilderness formula. I
came to see that here was a way of life as necessary and as deeply
rooted in some men as the love of home and family, a vital cultural aspect of life which brought happiness and lasting content.

The idea of wilderness enjoyment is not new. Through our literature we find abundant reference to it, but seldom of the virile, masculine type of experience men need today. Since the beginning of time poets have sung of the healing power of solitude and of communion with nature, but for them the wilderness meant the joys of contemplation. Typical of this tone of interpretation is Thoreau with his "tonic of wildness," but to the men I have come to know his was an understanding that did not begin to cover what they feel. To him, the wild meant the pastoral meadows of Concord and Walden Pond, and the joy he had, though unmistakably genuine, did not approach the fierce, unquenchable desire of my men today. For them the out-of-doors is not enough; nor are the delights of meditation. They need the sense of actual struggle and accomplishment, where the odds are real and where they know that they are no longer playing make believe. These men need more than picnics, purling streams, or fields of daffodils to stifle their discontent, more than mere solitude and contemplation to give them peace.

Burroughs, another lover of the out-of-doors, spoke often of the wilderness, but knew it not at all. When he regretted having to leave Old Slabsides on the Hudson for the wilds of Alaska and the West, we knew there was little of the primitive urge in his nature. The birds, the common phenomena of the passing seasons, and work in his vineyard satisfied abundantly his need of reality and physical contact with the earth. For him the wild had little charm. As we explore our literature for men who have felt deeply about wilderness we find them few indeed, perhaps because in the past there was wilderness enough and men had not learned to wean themselves so completely away from its influence. Invariably men wrote of the struggle and the dominating effect of wilderness as a mighty unconquered force and everywhere we find evidence of the part it played in molding the lives of those it touched. Fear was the keynote of the past, fear of the brooding monster of the unknown, and little of the joy of adventure and freedom is ever in evidence. Were it not for a few such daring souls as Joseph Conrad and Jack London, we would know little of the feeling some men have for the far places of the earth.

With the rapid elimination of the frontiers, due to increased facility of transportation and huge development programs, the opportunity to see and know real wilderness has become increasingly difficult. As it approaches the status of rarity for the first time in history, we see it not as something to be feared and subdued, not as an encumbrance to the advance of civilization, but instead as a distinctly cultural asset which contributes to spiritual satisfaction. The greater part of the old wilderness is gone, but during the centuries in which we fought our way through it we unconsciously absorbed its influence. Now as conquering invaders, we feel the need of the very elements which a short time ago we fought to eradicate. The wild has left its mark upon us and now that we have succeeded in surrounding ourselves with a complexity of new and often unnatural habits of daily living, we long for the old stimulus which only the unknown could give.

Why wilderness? No two men would have the same explanation. Something definite does happen to most men, however, when they hit the out trails of our last frontiers, and though they react in various ways there is a certain uniformity noticeable to one who has often seen them make the break with civilization. Whatever it is they are changed almost overnight from the prosaic conformists they may have been, who dress, think, and act like all the rest, to adventurers ready to die with their boots on, explorers pushing into the blue, once more members of a pioneering band.

It is surprising how quickly a man sheds the habiliments of civilization and how soon he feels at home in the wilds. Before many days have passed, he feels that the life he has been living was merely an interruption in a long wilderness existence and that now again he is back at the real business of living. And when we think of the comparatively short time that we have been living and working as we do now, when we recall that many of us are hardly a generation removed from the soil, and that a scant few thousand years ago our ancestors roamed and hunted the fastnesses of Europe, it is not strange that the smell of woodsmoke and the lure of the primitive is with us yet. Racial memory is a tenacious thing, and for some it is always easy to slip back into the deep grooves of the past. What we feel most deeply are those things which as a race we have been doing the longest, and the hunger men feel for the wilds and a roving life is natural evidence of the need of repeating a plan of existence that for untold centuries was common practice. It is still in our blood and many more centuries must pass before we loose much of its hold.

Civilized living in the great towns, with all their devices for comfort and convenience, is far too sudden a violation of slowly changing racial habit and we find that what gave men pleasure in the past—simple, primitive tasks and the ordinary phenomena of life in the open—today give the same satisfaction. Men have found at last that there is a penalty for too much comfort and ease, a penalty of lassitude and inertia and the frustrated feeling that goes with unreality. Certainly the adjustment for many has been difficult and it is those who must ever so often break their bonds and hie themselves away.

All do not feel the need and there are many perfectly content with life as they find it. They will always be the picnickers and the strollers, and for them are highways, gravelled trails, and country clubs. For them scenic vistas of the wild from the shelter of broad and cool verandas. The others, those who cannot rest, are of a different breed. For them is sweat and toil, hunger and thirst, and the fierce satisfaction that only comes with hardship.

While wilderness means escape from the perplexing problems of everyday life and freedom from the tyranny of wires, bells, schedules, and pressing responsibility, nevertheless, it may be at first a decided shock and days and even weeks may pass before men are finally aware that the tension is gone. When the realization does come, they experience a peace of mind and relaxation which a short time before would have seemed impossible. With this dramatic change of atmosphere comes an equally dramatic change in individual reactions as they feel that the need of front and reserve is gone.

I have seen staid educators, dignified surgeons, congressmen, and admirals tie up their heads in gaudy bandannas, go shirtless to bring on the tan of the northern sun, and wear bowie knives in their belts. I have seen them glory in the muck of portages, fight the crashing combers on stormy lakes with the abandon of boys on their first adventure. I have heard them laugh as they haven't laughed for years and bellow old songs in the teeth of a gale. With their new found freedom and release many things become important that were half forgotten—sunsets, the coloring of clouds and leaves, reflections in the water. I can honestly say, that I have heard more laughter in a week out there than in any month in town. Men laugh and sing as naturally as breathing once the strain is gone.

With escape comes perspective. Far from the towns and all they denote, engrossed in their return to the old habits of wilderness living, men begin to wonder if the speed and pressure they have left are not a little senseless. Here where matters of food, shelter, rest, and new horizons are all important, they begin to question the worthwhileness of their old objectives. Now they have long days with nothing to clutter their minds but the simple problems of wilderness living, and at last they have time to think. Then comes the transformation and, of a sudden, they are back to earth. Things move slowly, majestically in the wilds and the coming of the full moon in itself becomes of major importance. Countless natural phenomena begin to show themselves, things long forgotten and needing only the rejuvenating experience of actual contact to bring them back. With this, some of the old primitive philosophy works itself into their thinking, and in their new calm they forget to worry. Their own affairs seem trivial. Perspective? I sometimes think that men go to the wilds for that alone. Finding it means equilibrium, the long-time point of view so often lost in towns.

Ernest Holt, one-time guard to the late Colonel Fawcett on

his first Amazon expedition, told me that in the depths of the
jungle he experienced a spiritual uplift and sense of oneness
with life that he could find nowhere else. I believe that here
is a sensation born of perspective that most men know in any
wilderness. Whenever it comes, men are conscious of a unity
with the primal forces of creation and all life that swiftly anni-
hilates the feeling of futility, frustration, and unreality. When
men realize that they are on their own, that if they are to be
sheltered and fed and, what is more, return to civilization, they
must depend entirely on their own ingenuity, everything they
do assumes tremendous importance. Back home, mistakes can
be made and easily excused or remedied, but here mistakes
might cause discomfort or catastrophe. Knowing this makes
all the difference in the world in a man's attitude toward the
commonplace activities of daily life. Simple duties like the
preparation of food, the taking of a fish, or the caching of supplies becomes fraught with import. Life soon develops a new
and fascinating angle and days which to the uninitiated may
seem humdrum or commonplace are filled with the adventure
of living for its own sake. There is no make-believe here, but
reality in the strictest sense of the word.

Men who have shared campfires together, who have known
the pinch of hunger and what it means to cut a final cigarette
in half two hundred miles from town, enjoy a comradeship
that others never know. Only at war or on wilderness expeditions can this type of association be found, and I believe that it
is this that men miss as much in civilized living as contact with
the wild itself. I know a busy surgeon who once left his hospi-
tal operating room and traveled without thought of compensation a thousand miles through the bitter cold of midwinter
to save the life of his guide, stricken with pneumonia. Nothing
could have made him consider deserting his practice to take
such a long hazardous trip but a call from a comrade in need.
I stood at the bedside of that woodsman as he babbled in-
coherently of rapids and lakes and wilderness camps they had
known together, and I knew then that here was a bond be-

tween men that could only be forged in the wilds, something deep and fine, something based on loyalty to open skies and distance and a way of life men need.

I do not advocate that the men of whom I speak allow the wilderness idea to claim all of their energy or enthusiasm. I do believe, however, that if for a short time each year it were possible for them to get away, not necessarily to the great wildernesses of the Arctic or the Canadian lakes, but to some wild part of the country which has not as yet been entirely caught up in some scheme of exploitation or development, that they would return to their friends and families strengthened and rejuvenated.

Why wilderness? Ask the men who have known it and who have made it part of their lives. They might not be able to explain, but your very question will kindle a light in eyes that have reflected the camp fires of a continent, eyes that have known the glory of dawns and sunsets and nights under the stars. Wilderness to them is real and this they do know; when the pressure becomes more than they can stand, somewhere back of beyond, where roads and steel and towns are still forgotten, they will find release.

American Forests, September 1938

Flying In

By the late 1930s, the advent of safe and reliable seaplanes made it possible to drop people into remote lakes deep in the wilderness for a few hours of fishing, and also made it profitable to build resorts on isolated tracts of private land on lakes within the federally designated roadless areas of Superior National Forest. By 1944, nine Ely-area resorts advertised fly-in fishing trips. To Sigurd, this spelled the beginning of the end for wilderness all over the country. He knew that wilderness flying would become a booming business after the world war ended, as pilots returned home and aircraft industries retooled excess factory machinery. Few people heeded him when he first voiced his concerns in 1940, but in 1945 he gave the issue national attention with his Sports Afield *article "Flying In."*

In the past, the largest tourism-related threat to wilderness had been new roads. Airplanes were far worse, immediately opening large swaths of wild land that previously had been accessible only to those traveling by foot, horse, or canoe. They also opened a new era in which wilderness defenders had to explain why the method of travel *was relevant to the meaning of wilderness. As one might expect, Sigurd raises issues of silence and solitude. But to him it is clearly more than that, and he gives a new twist to his earlier statements about the physical aspects of the wilderness experience. More than a third of the article consists of his opening anecdote in which*

he describes his own fly-in trip to a lake in the heart of the wilder-
ness, and the vague dissatisfaction he felt despite spending time at a
favorite campsite. Flying in, he concludes, makes it much harder to
feel the same kind of connectedness to the wild one experiences when
doing the intimate and hard work of paddling and portaging.

"Flying In" was the forty-six-year-old junior college dean's most
prominent issue-related article to date, and marked the beginning
of his eventual ascendancy to the front ranks of the national con-
servation movement, which would occur in the next few years as
he spearheaded the successful fight to ban airplanes from the canoe
country wilderness.

❋ ❋ ❋

Roaring along at 3,000 feet, it seemed to me that
until then I had traveled like a mole, burrowing through the
timber and brush of portages, creeping slowly down the rivers
and over wind-roughened lakes, my vision a mole's vision limited by trees and rocks and rushes with never a vista of more
than the water that bore my canoe. But now, for the first time,
I saw it as a whole, the wilderness lake country I had explored
in the past. From this height I saw the Superior National Forest
as a hawk might see it, the blue and green lacework of sprawl-
ing lakes and their connecting rivers, the level green lawns of
muskeg and the tufted roughness of spruce and pine on the
uplands. This was new and exciting, different from the close,
intimate years when I had known the intricate maze of canoe
trails as a mole in its near blindness might know the turnings
of its own runways in the turf.

To the east lay Gabemichigami, my destination, to the south,
the white, brawling Kawishowa, to the north the dark virgin
timber of the Quetico, behind me, 20 hurtling, noise-packed
minutes, the pavements of the town I had left. The entire country seemed in flood, the network of interminable waterways
running one into the other, filling all the valleys with their blue
and green, every sunken spot between the hills.

I glanced at the map and saw that just ahead was Gabemichigami, a tremendous gash between two steep ridges. The plane banked, circled, and then, like the hawk it was, dropped to its kill, spiraling downward until it swooped close over the reaching tops of the pine trees. It sideslipped between the towering shores and in a moment the pontoons were slapping the water and the plane nosed gently toward shore.

The pilot threw out my pack and I scrambled along the pontoon and jumped for the landing. A farewell push and the wings turned toward the open lake once more. The engine roared and the plane moved out in a cloud of spray. A minute later and it was in the air over the ridges heading back toward town. I looked at my watch. Thirty minutes since we had left and here I was alone, deep in the heart of the wilderness at a point that normally would have taken me three days of hard travel by portage and canoe. I sat down and pondered, trying to believe it.

After the quiet had returned, I looked around me, found my old campsite just as I had left it a year ago. The balsam boughs were dry and withered over my bed and the pothooks still in place over the fireplace. There was the same little creek tumbling down from the rocks in its escape from Little Saganaga to the east, there the same swirling pool with its trout. I had dreamed of this spot, had lain awake at night thinking about it, picturing each indelible memory, thinking how wonderful it would be to spend a whole day there all alone and taking once again some of those beautiful brown trout below the riffles. It was then I decided to fly in, for there was no time during the war for extended and leisurely canoe trips. And I would see the old wilderness in a new way and steal from the future one more glimpse of one of the most beautiful spots I knew. Now, to my utter amazement, the dream had come true.

At first I couldn't realize the change, so violent had it been. Formerly, with days of travel behind me, by the time I had reached this spot on the map the country had had a chance to soak in and become a part of me, but as I stood listening to the far drone of the plane I realized I was still part of the environment I had left and that it would take time for the old feeling of being one with the wilderness to come.

I strolled back over the portage to the dead water above the rapids, sat there a long time trying to recapture the feeling of satisfaction and accomplishment I had known the last time in, but all that came to me was the violent throbbing reaction to my flight and a jumble made up of the many things I had done in the last hour of preparation. There was no uplift, as of old.

When the tent was up, fresh boughs cut for my bed, I busied myself with my rod and began to cast for trout. Before long I had a fine three-pounder, one of the golden brown trout with reddish fins that grow to their best in Gabemichigami. I caught three all told and for an hour knew the excitement of playing real wilderness trout on light tackle; and what grand fish they were, hard and firm and full of fight as they always are in the spring when still in the shallow water. That hour it seemed to me was worth all of the waiting I had done in the past.

But that night in front of my fire, listening to the loons and their echoing calls from Little Saganaga, Kakequabic, Ogishge-muncie, and other lakes around, I knew that something was wrong with the way I felt. This was what I had dreamed of doing for months, but for the first time in my life I had failed to work for the joy of knowing the wilderness, for the first time I had not given it a chance to soak into my consciousness and become a part of me.

True, I had seen the country, all of it and far more than I might ever see on an ordinary trip, I had caught my trout and I was now at the very place of my dreams. It had been fun, every second of it, but I realized then that something was lacking, something gone that was there before when it had taken three days or more of portaging over rocks and windfalls and muskeg, 50 miles of bending to the paddle and fighting the wind, three campsites in the wild behind me, but always the great goal ahead—the prettiest campsite in the border country. That vision alone had been enough to make the packs light and to take the sting from tired muscles. The mere thought of that camp with its trout, the creek singing its way beside it and the feeling that there was the very heart and soul of the wilderness had been compensation enough. Then, when my tent was pitched on Gabemichigami, I knew the real joy and happiness that only the wild can give.

The next afternoon, the plane roared again over the horizon and in half an hour I was back to the pavements, the automobiles, and my friends. Yes, I had been on a flight, had been far in the wilderness, had taken some good trout, in short had enjoyed myself, but I was still somewhat out of breath, still somewhat baffled by what I had done. It had certainly been worthwhile seeing the country from the air, the flight had given me a bird's-eye view and perspective that I could have gotten in no other way and the beauty was not lost on me; but the next time, I knew, if I was ever to recapture the real satisfaction I had known in the past, I would have to go back to the old way with pack and canoe and work myself to the bone. I would have to be a mole again and learn once more the feel of rocks under my feet, breathe the scent of balsam and spruce under the sun, feel the wetness and spray of waterways, the spring of muskeg, be a part of the wilderness itself, not merely an onlooker. Then and only then would the old feeling return.

Since then, however, I have made many flights into the interior hunting and fishing areas of the Canadian Border country. I feel that I have really gotten to know the country by air. I realize, too, the thrill of going in that way and I have come to know hundreds of men who have done the same thing and am familiar with their reaction. Invariably their reaction is the same as mine, that the way to get the real wallop out of the wilderness is not to fly into it but to go by the old primitive means of travel. Of course, this does not rule out flying to the fringes of the wilds, and proceeding on your own from there.

If it were only a matter of getting game or fish, there would be no argument. But living in the wilderness is far more than just getting your limit, far more than being able to say you have been in the wilds. It is an intangible something compounded of the countless intimacies a man has with his surroundings when he is on his own. To many men wilderness living is an inherent need, a heritage of the days when their forefathers were a part of it. For them it is a primal necessity to every so often get back into the old racial grooves of experience.

If it were merely a matter of choice, if it were up to each individual outdoorsman to decide what was best for him personally and there was plenty of country for all, then there would be nothing to worry about. But that doesn't happen to be the problem.

For the first time in its history, America is faced with the possibility of losing the few remaining bits of wilderness left over from the pioneering days. That time is now, and sportsmen, wilderness travelers, and sight-seers, whether they like to travel into the back country by plane, canoe, pack horse, or on foot, must decide immediately what they want. There is little time left for reflection and the weighing of values. The fate of every wilderness region on the continent is at stake.

We all know what is coming. A man would have to be blind not to see it. We are on the verge of a new era, an era of flight when planes will be as commonplace as automobiles are now. Great bases have been built all over the country, even in the far north, and thousands of landing strips are planned by towns everywhere for postwar construction. At the close of hostilities, several hundred thousand highly trained pilots will return to civilian pursuits. With them will come other hundreds of thousands of skilled aviation mechanics, technicians, and men trained in the services of administration and supply, men who hope to make aviation their careers. Industries now building planes for war will speedily convert to peacetime manufacture and within a few years the skies of America will be alive with ships of all kinds. The family plane is now a reality and the helicopter ready for production. The dream of a plane for every home, of safe flying for young and old, is no longer a wild prophecy. It is reality.

Flying is here and it is here to stay. We can no more hold it back than we could have stopped the development of the automobile 30 years ago and we do not want to hold it back even if we could, as it will without question be the greatest boon to the progress of mankind in the history of civilization. We know now that within a decade or two there will be such an increase in flying that the present or the prewar era will seem like the early 1900s in the development of the automobile.

That is the overall picture of what is to come and the day is not far distant when, outside of the National Parks, there will be no extensive wilderness regions that cannot be penetrated. And it will not be long before people will discover that it is possible to take a wilderness trip without the expense, physical hardship, and time involved in the past. Naturally they will want to experience the sort of swift expedition I enjoyed into Gabemichigami, the sort of thing they had thought impossible before. For them a whole field of adventure is wide open and beckoning for the first time.

They will want to enjoy the thrills the helicopter fans talk about, spend a week end camping in some lonely alpine meadow at timber line where the trout really take a fly and that without the hazard and expense of a pack trip through the mountains; they will want to drop into one of the countless little lakes far up in the Canadian wilds that heretofore could only be reached by days of paddling and packing; they will want to hunt for moose and deer and caribou where men have never hunted before or land at the headwaters of trout streams that have always defied them in the past.

All of that is now held before them. For the first time the wilderness is accessible to all who wish to enjoy it, and we know that there will soon be no spot on the face of the earth that will not be invaded. The lakes of the canoe country will have planes on every bit of water big enough for a landing and takeoff. Every mountain meadow will see the helicopters dropping in. Roadless and wilderness areas set aside by the U.S. Forest Service for the express purpose of preserving a few remnants of the old America for those who wish to enjoy the wilderness way of life will be a mockery. Within a decade or two the wilderness will be gone and no area will be left where a man can find solitude.

Physically, of course, the wilderness will still be there and hunting and fishing will continue for a long time to come, but spiritually the old wilderness will disappear, for the real wild is a place not only where there is game and fish and natural vegetation but also where there is the atmosphere of the primitive. It is a place where men can find the release from civilized living that has been denied them in towns, a place where they can know the comradeship and closeness with nature that comes only when they are a part of it and live and travel as men lived and traveled in the past. That is what we shall lose; that is what all devotees of the wilderness way of life dread once flying really begins.

I have seen it happen within a year, know what it means to be on a lake deep in the back country, a lake that has taken you and your party days to reach, only to have a plane drop in beside you with a cargo of fishermen fresh from the cities down below. Until that moment the wilderness belonged to you and you had known the deep and abiding satisfaction that comes only when you are far removed from civilization and on your own. But with the arrival of the plane all of that vanished.

If these men had come in by pack and canoe as we had, we would have greeted them joyfully, shared with them everything we had and made a real celebration, but all we felt was a deep and smoldering resentment born of the realization that they hadn't worked to get in, hadn't, it seemed, earned the right to real wilderness enjoyment. What did they know of portages and rapids and packing and bucking a head wind? How could they possibly know the thrill of reaching a goal under their own power? Somehow we all felt that they hadn't paid to get in, had in a sense crashed the gates and were getting something for nothing.

This may sound absolutely unreasonable to those who have never had the experience, might seem to smack of the rankest selfishness and lack of understanding. But I have guided enough men through the wilds to know their reactions to this sort of thing. I know how they feel, know they want room and solitude and a lot of it without crowding or interference. I have been with them too long to be wrong about them. These men are the real wilderness men of the continent and I firmly believe that as such they are as much entitled to a preservation of the kind of experience they enjoy as the fliers are entitled to theirs.

Now if there were only a handful of wilderness men who felt this way there would still be no problem as it is possible even in a democracy to deprive the minority if it is in the interest of the greater public good. But I know there are hundreds of thousands of men, young and old, who still feel strongly that wilderness living of the old type is something that should be preserved. In the armed forces all over the world are young men who are dreaming of the days when they will return and again enjoy the back country they have known and it is up to us here to keep our faith with them and do what we can to save their precious heritage from complete annihilation.

The only hope of preserving a few remnants of the old wilderness for these men is to work out a comprehensive zoning plan in which the entire country will be classified as to the type of recreational land use it is best suited for. Huge areas can be opened to aviation, areas in which the highest values are not supremely of the type adapted to the old methods of primitive travel, but it is no more than right that a few of the superlative regions exemplified by the lakes of the canoe country or the high country of pack trips in our National Forests be set aside forever for primitive travel only. Such areas, which represent the last remaining examples of the real wilderness of the United States, should not be flown over or penetrated by planes but should be protected by having all aircraft land only at designated boundary points. This surely can be done without great hardship to those who wish to fly in, for the areas in question are a pitifully small proportion of the greater areas available for such use.

Naturally there will be exceptions to be worked out for regions that have long been served by aircraft without any serious impairment of their primitive values. Such areas might still be served within definite limits. It might also be possible to open up certain other regions in a system of rotation, but whatever is worked out, the paramount need today is for some workable plan of regulation that will preserve the very thing all men, fliers and nonfliers, want to enjoy, the experience of seeing new and unspoiled country.

It would seem wise, in view of the tremendous stake involved, to appoint an advisory board in each State composed of sportsmen, scientists, and representatives of the Forest Service, National Park Service, and Conservation Department, men who understand the values involved and who could work out an unbiased solution for the problems of each particular area. This board could submit its findings to a National Aeronautics Board for approval and action and this in turn could promote proper legislation.

At the present time there is no plan even though we all know what the future will bring, and I believe I speak for millions of men when I say they view the possible end of the American wilderness with alarm. There is no quarrel with those who look forward to flying into the wilds. Theirs is a legitimate desire and a man would have to be pretty senile if the thought of such an expedition did not thrill him. But we must admit that if we permitted unrestricted indulgence of this desire, we would soon deprive ourselves of the very thing we would now exploit and, what is possibly more important, we shall most certainly deprive posterity of one of its most precious heritages, the right to know and enjoy the wilderness ways of its forefathers.

Sports Afield, September 1945

We Need Wilderness

Sometime in the early 1940s Devereux Butcher, the fiery executive director of the National Parks Association (NPA), discovered Sigurd's 1938 American Forests *article, "Why Wilderness?" In 1944 he asked Sigurd to write a similar article for* National Parks Magazine, *and the result, published during Sigurd's postwar year in Europe as a teacher for the U.S. Army, was his strongest statement yet on behalf of undisturbed nature. Butcher liked it so much that he not only had the NPA reprint five thousand copies to begin sending to all new members but also included a condensed version of it in the NPA's book* Exploring Our National Parks, *released in 1947 by Oxford University Press with an initial run of twenty thousand copies. Other organizations also reprinted the article, and on May 5, 1947, NPA field secretary Fred Packard wrote to Sigurd, "Probably no other article that has been published in the* National Parks Magazine *has had so wide an effect."*

Writing at the end of a long and terrible world war, Sigurd focuses on the role of wilderness in rejuvenating the human spirit. Never again would he spend as much time on the physical aspects of the wilderness experience as he did in his earlier articles. While he admits that wilderness "does play an important recreational role," he maintains that "its real function will always be as a spiritual backlog in the high speed mechanical world in which we live."

For the first time, Sigurd brings up the topic of the importance of wilderness for study and scientific research—and he does so only to dismiss it, or at least to dismiss those who want to preserve wilderness for this purpose only, without understanding its spiritual value. For the first time, Sigurd writes that some people "can find their wilderness in tiny hidden corners" in the middle of a large city, and in writing this at least implicitly shows the importance of preserving not only the remaining large areas of wild land far from the cities but the small green spaces where most Americans live. And for the first time, using an anecdote about Canadian humorist Stephen Leacock as evidence, he argues that the large wilderness areas are important not only to the people who travel through them but to many others whose lives are enriched merely by knowing these areas still exist.

Sigurd would revisit this article a decade later, using pieces of it—including the Leacock anecdote—in the final essay of his 1958 book, Listening Point.

❅ ❅ ❅

A FLEET OF ROCKY, PINE-CRESTED ISLANDS floats between us and the western horizon. It is dusk in the wilderness, a time of quiet and sunset-colored waters. The white tents are pale against the dark forest. Canoes are overturned on the shore, beds made, all equipment under cover, everything snug for the night. In the calm air the smoke from our dying supper fire rises straight into the sky. A loon calls and is answered from a lake over the hills. For a moment the timbered ridges echo and re-echo with their wild notes.

A week ago we had left the steel. One of my party was the head of a great corporation in Chicago, another a well-known surgeon from New York, and the third a judge from Washington, D.C. They had come north to get the feeling of wilderness, to renew companionships and associations almost forgotten during the mad rush of the war years. Like many others I have guided on wilderness expeditions, these were men in their prime, highly successful in their professions, suave and cultured; but they were fatigued and worn by responsibilities in the great cities. Now they wanted to have fun. They wanted to forget for a while the enmeshing tentacles of civilization and industry, and for a few weeks to feel that old freedom they used to know. In camp each night they sat near the water's edge and talked until dark.

"Queer," said the judge, "to think that a thousand miles south of us, people are rushing around just as busily as the day we left. Somehow up here it doesn't make sense."

"Yes," said the corporation head, "I can see the Chicago Loop this very moment with people pouring madly out of their burrows and heading for some place else just as we'll be doing again in a week or two. From here, Chicago and New York and Washington and the other cities seem like gigantic anthills. But every person in them has a purpose in life, or thinks he has; yet, to me, as we sit here amid this beauty, their endless rushing, or at least the speed with which they move, appears foolish."

"What gets me," replied the surgeon, "is the peace and quiet up here. In the big hospitals a man is apt to forget that there is anything but tension in the world. You come back here, and the tension is gone. The world is quiet and peaceful again, and there is no pressure."

"You're right," agreed the judge. "It's good just to know that a place like this exists. When I get all tied up in a knot over some legal problem, I'll shut my eyes and remember."

"And when I sit in at my next board of directors meeting," said the man of affairs, "and try to explain what's happened to a block of stock or a contract that hasn't been going too well, I'll recall how we sat on this rock, and I'll remember how little difference it all makes in the long run."

"Two weeks from now when the operating rooms have been working overtime," mused the doctor, "and I've been flying from Chicago to New York, and my brain is whirling with speed, I'm going to think of those loons. They'll still be calling, no matter where I am. Yes, just the memory of them will be good medicine for me."

I watched these men for a week. Now freed of mental strain,
taking vigorous, pleasurable exercise, and breathing pure air
twenty-four hours a day, they became normal human beings
with much of the spirit of the carefree boy about them. These,
my companions on a wilderness cruise, had again discovered
how a man can find release; where he can recapture his perspective and the calm of untroubled years; where he can shed
responsibilities and know the meaning of freedom and the joys
of simple living. They, like others I have known on wilderness
expeditions of the past, have found it here. The untouched
rivers and forests and lakes were the answer. Now they could
return to the cities with peace in their hearts.

With the coming of twilight, hermit thrushes were singing
in the hills behind us. From a near-by cove came the disturbed
quacking of a mallard hen, then a splash, and a pair of mallards
whistled overhead. A moose was the cause of their disturbance.
We saw him wade into the shallows to feed on water lily plants
there.

Soon the evening star came out and hung like a lantern in
the sky. The hermits were silent now, but a few white-throats
sounded their clear notes back in the hills. The turbulent world
of civilization was far away. Noisy, dirty, bustling cities, like
nightmares, seemed no part of reality.

According to Webster, wilderness is a trackless waste un-
inhabited by man. To the people of America, as typified by
the men who were with me on this particular trip, it is far
more than that. It is something so closely tied up with their
traditions, so tightly woven into their cultural backgrounds,
their emotions, and philosophies of life, that it cannot be ig-
nored or neglected.

*Wilderness to the people of America is a spiritual necessity, an
antidote to the high pressure of modern life, a means of regaining
serenity and equilibrium.*

I have found that people go to the wilderness for many things,
but the most important of these is perspective. They may think
they go for the fishing or the scenery or companionship, but in

reality it is something far deeper. They go to the wilderness for the good of their souls. I sometimes feel as though they had actually gone to another planet from which they can watch with cool detachment the fierce and sometimes meaningless scurryings of their kind. Then when the old philosophy of earth-oneness begins to return to them, they slowly realize that once again they are in tune with sun and stars and all natural things, and with that knowledge comes happiness and contentment.

I believe this need of wilderness is inherent in most of us, even those seemingly farthest removed from it by civilized living. The cities may cover it up, make us forget temporarily; but deep underneath is an inherent urge for naturalness and simplicity and a way of life different from the one we know.

Henry Thoreau sensed this need of mankind when he said, "We can never have enough of nature. We must be refreshed by the sight of vast and titanic features—the wilderness with its living and decaying trees. We need to witness our own limits transgressed and some life pasturing freely where we never wander."

There is a school of thought that considers wilderness solely as an opportunity for nature study and scientific research and sees no spiritual value in the effect of wild country on those who come in contact with it. These people lack vision, for if they understood the primary purpose of the accumulation of knowledge generally, they would know that unless such effort results in furthering man's sense of companionship and understanding of the earth, and thereby contributes to his spiritual contentment and happiness, it has not achieved its purpose.

There is another group made up of practical minded individuals who see no sense in setting aside an area for esthetic or recreational purposes. This group considers wilderness devotees as irresponsible wildlifers who have gone off the deep end in their enthusiasm for the out-of-doors. They look at the last remaining bits of primitive America as a final opportunity to "get rich quick" in the best pioneer tradition. They are the ones who would dam Yellowstone Lake, cut the last sequoias, and convert the canoe country of the Quetico-Superior into a huge storage reservoir. To them the wilderness has no other value than the practical, and they think it criminal for resources to stand commercially unused. They also need the wilderness, but their need is blinded by greed.

There is a third group larger than all the rest. That is the great mass of recreation-minded Americans who see in the wilderness not an opportunity for exploitation or for the furtherance of knowledge, but rather as an opportunity to satisfy a vital spiritual deficiency within themselves. They are the ones who head into the wilderness regions because they must. Wilderness to them is a tonic, a panacea for nervousness and monotony. They go to it once a month or once a year as a sick man might go to his physician. These people know that wilderness to them is a necessity if they are to keep their balance.

To place a value on wilderness is as difficult as to speak of the value of a landmark or an heirloom in terms of money. There are certain things that cannot be evaluated because of their emotional appeal. Wilderness is in this category. While a certain area might have worth as a museum piece, or because of certain economic factors, its real worth will always depend upon how people feel about it and what it does for them. If it contributes to spiritual welfare, if it gives them perspective and a sense of oneness with mountains, forests, or waters, or in any way at all enriches their lives, then the area is beyond price. It is as hard to place a true value on wilderness as it is to decide what type of wild country is the best. What one man needs and finds satisfying, might not be at all what another requires. In the final analysis each man knows within himself what it is he wants, and in each case his choice is tempered by his own past, his dreams and memories, his hopes for the future, and his ability to enjoy.

Some can find their wildernesses in tiny hidden corners where, through accident rather than design, man has saved just a breath of the primeval America. I know of a glen in the heart of a great city park system, a tiny roaring canyon where many seeking solitude and beauty can find release. It is dark in there, and damp, and in the heat of the summer it is cool. Ferns and lichens and liverworts cling to the rocks, and there grow flowers that thrive only in the shadows where the air is charged with mist. The water swirls through this canyon as it has for thousands of years, and the sounds are the sounds of a land far removed from civilization. A highway runs within a hundred yards and cars pass almost overhead, but the rocks and trees screen it from view and the only evidence of traffic is a vague hum that blends with the whisper of the wind and the music of rushing water. There, if a man wishes, he can regain in a swift moment the feeling of the wild, and steal, for a brief instant, respite from the noise and confusion of a big city. There, if he has perspective, he may recharge his soul.

There are men, however, who crave action and distance and far horizons beyond the steel. No little sanctuaries for them along the fringes of civilization. They must know wild country and all that goes with it, must feel the bite of a tumpline on the portages, the desperate battling against waves on stormy lakes. They must know hunger and thirst and privation and the companionship men know only on the out trails of the world. When, after days of paddling and packing, they find themselves on some bare glaciated point a hundred miles from town and stand there gazing down a great wilderness waterway, listening to the loons and seeing the wild rocky islands floating in the sunset, they, too, know the meaning of communion with nature.

Another finds his wilderness in the mountains of the West. There, camped in some high alpine meadow, with the horses grazing quietly along an ice-fed glacial stream, jagged peaks towering above him into the snow-capped summits of some mighty range, and all about him the beauty and grandeur of the high country, he finds his particular ultimate. To him such a setting is the primitive on a noble scale—there a timelessness that can never be approached elsewhere. The very bigness of the landscape gives him a sense of personal contact with immensity and space. He comes down from his mountains, as all men have since the beginning of time, refreshed spiritually and ready again for the complexities of life among his kind.

There are those who say that only in the great swamps and flowages of the deep South, in the flooded cypress stands and mangroves, or along the deltas and savannas of the rivers, can one understand what wilderness really is. And in a sense they are right, for it was in such places that life supposedly evolved. Some men may sense instinctively that there conditions more closely approximate the primeval phases of the earth's history than anywhere else. If it is purely the atmosphere of the wild that counts, then surely there a man might get a closer feeling with the past and the future than in any other wilderness.

Stephen Leacock, when asked why he persisted in living in Toronto instead of returning to his beloved England, replied that he liked living in Toronto because it was so close to the wilderness of Hudson Bay, that the very thought of the thousands of miles of barren country to the north gave him a sense of spaciousness and adventure that did him good. In that statement he voiced the feeling of thousands of people who, like him, though they may never penetrate the back country, nevertheless enjoy the feeling of living close to it. For these the wilderness is just as much an inspiration as for those who travel through it by horse, canoe, dogteam, or other primitive means. The very awareness of it gives to them that feeling of the frontier characteristic of all jumping-off places. In such regions the air itself seems rarified and charged with something different that Thoreau might have called, "the early morning fragrance of the wild."

Whatever their type and wherever they are found, be these wilderness places large or small, mountains, lakes, deserts, swamps, or forests, they do fill a vital need. Gradually wilderness has become a cultural necessity to us, the people of America, and while it does play an important recreational role, its real function will always be as a spiritual backlog in the high speed mechanical world in which we live. We have discovered that the presence of wilderness in itself is a balance wheel and an aid to equilibrium.

City life is artificial. Because artificiality leads to a sense of unreality and frustration, unhappiness often results. That is the price a people pays for high technological success, and that is the reason an intelligent, thinking people knows that unless it can break away and renew its contact with a slow-moving natural philosophy, it will lose its perspective and forget simplicity and wholesomeness.

Most Americans are not far removed from their pioneer ancestry, are still close enough to the covered wagon days and the era of backwoods settlements and farms, so that they remember, more than sense, what they have lost. And being so close, it is not at all surprising that when production lines and speed and synthetic living seem more than they can bear, they instinctively head back to the wilderness where they know everything will be all right. Once returned to the old ways of living, their serenity comes back and they find that their capacity for enjoyment has not changed. That is what the wilderness means to America.

In recognition of this now almost general need of our people, the National Park Service, the U.S. Forest Service, and the various states have wisely set aside many areas that may be classed as wilderness—areas dedicated to the spiritual welfare of all. They vary in size from the three million acre Salmon River Wilderness Area of Idaho, a region large enough for a man to travel for days without crossing his own tracks, to areas only a few square miles in extent—museum bits of the once vast primeval wilderness of North America.

Far-sighted conservationists have fought hasty developmental programs that had as their goal the exploitation of the few remaining sections of wilderness. Sometimes they have won, but more often they have lost, due to the fact that, as a people, Americans still do not realize the importance of wilderness preservation as an investment in future happiness.

The idea that America is a land of freedom and limitless opportunity is perhaps responsible for our lethargy in saving more of the wild than we have. A few short decades ago wilderness was something that had to be fought and overcome, the one great hindrance to the opening and development of the continent. We remember the pioneer days when the great plantations of pine were stripped and burned, when huge reclamation projects drained swamps and lowered the water tables to the danger point, when power projects were thought the only legitimate uses of streams. The old destructive "cut out and get out" philosophy of those days is still very much alive in our thinking, so that it is not surprising to find many who even now view the few wilderness regions we have set aside as a challenge to move in and make a fortune in spite of the outraged sentiment of those who do see their value.

We see these interests constantly at work backed by powerful lobbies, interests which call for the cutting of the last stands of virgin timber, the exploitation of the last untouched reserves of the continent. They make the preservation of any section of wild country a constant battle, and place the comparatively small reservations we have set aside, in constant jeopardy. The existence of this element in our population makes necessary the utmost vigilance on the part of governmental agencies in charge of the administration of our parks and forests, as well as on the part of those organizations scattered throughout the land that understand what is at stake. The reservations already created are woefully inadequate to meet the need and give to the people of all parts of the United States the opportunity of wilderness recreation. This is especially true in the large centers of population; yet it is here that the need is greatest and opposition strongest.

One highly encouraging aspect of the wilderness problem is the realization that as a nation we are approaching cultural maturity. No young nation ever worries overmuch about the intangible assets of wilderness as long as its great battle is to subdue wilderness and carve out cities and roads and farms from the wild. Now, for the first time, we are able to look back and see where our mistakes and short-sighted policies have brought us; and at long last we are slowly emerging from the old pioneer concept that governed our thinking for the past three centuries. We can see that we have squandered a national heritage of beauty and wealth and have only a few places left to remind us of the continent's past primeval glory.

We know now just how valuable these fragments of the old America have become to us as a people. We see them now in a new light and realize that in addition to being museum pieces of the past, they are vital to our happiness and investments in national character. We also know that if we are to retain our contentment and balance, then we must never lose our contact with the earth, never forget the pioneer traditions of independence and resourcefulness under primitive conditions, never for a moment exchange the philosophy of the backwoods settler and Indian fighter for the comparative ease of the modern city. To give the people of this country an opportunity to renew their old associations as a race, to find themselves and their real qualities, to rejuvenate their spirits through simple living in the out-of-doors, is the real purpose of the preservation of wilderness.

National Parks Magazine, January–March 1946

The Preservation of Wilderness

This article illustrates the major arguments for preserving wilder-
ness in the early postwar era. Sigurd once again shows his concern
for the spiritual and psychological benefits of wilderness, but he also
describes economic, patriotic, historical, and scientific reasons for
preserving it.

When he mentioned scientific arguments for wilderness pre-
servation in his 1946 article "We Need Wilderness," he dismissed
them as detracting from the more important spiritual aspects. Now
he makes the scientific arguments part of his overall arsenal against
those who would destroy the wild for economic gain. Perhaps he
was responding to the new pressures wilderness faced in the boom-
ing postwar economy, including exponentially increasing visits to
national parks and other wild areas. One often gets the sense in
this and other pro-wilderness articles of the time that the writers
are trying to use any arguments they can that might help stem the
tide. The language of dollars and cents ruled political discourse,
and Sigurd, who clearly believed the spiritual and other intangible
values of wilderness were most important, nevertheless tries to give
fellow conservationists reasons for preserving wilderness that might
convince people who placed little weight in his most heartfelt points,
and that might bolster the opinions of those who did.

Wilderness preservation is far more than the setting aside of recreational areas for the pleasure of the few or satisfying those in search of the esthetic or the unusual. Its preservation is directly concerned with the physical and spiritual welfare of our people, their economy, their education, and their scientific progress. Such areas in addition bestow upon us the unique privilege of evaluating the present in the light of the past. In the words of Harvey Broome:

> These are islands in time with nothing to date them in the calendar of mankind. In these areas it is as though a person were looking backward into the ages and forward untold years. Here are bits of eternity.

Wilderness areas are museum pieces of primitive America, large enough so that one may travel perhaps for several days without coming in contact with any evidence of civilization. Removed from established lines of modern transportation, all travel is by foot, canoe, or by horse. Isolation is a major requirement.

Such regions must of necessity be surrounded by buffer zones to protect them from outside influences, insulating strips of country wide enough to absorb the shocks of contact from the outside world. Without them, wilderness values are easily disturbed. Solitude and the spirit of the wild cannot be preserved without complete protection.

The conception of wilderness today is entirely different from what it was a generation or two ago. When Americans first entered this continent, they came with bare hands, faced a vast unconquerable force, knowing that only by the grace of God and their own courage could they survive. To them it was a threat, an implacable power against which they were forced to pit their own puny efforts, a condition of existence with no compromise. It was something to be overcome, to be tamed and molded to their needs.

Today, with most of the continent developed, we see our remaining reserves in the light of adventure and enjoyment, as opportunities for education and scientific research, though in far too many cases as a final chance for exploitation. We survey these last remnants as conquerors survey the lands of former foes. The great threat has been overcome, the once wild continent subdued. We, the unquestioned masters, can bend what is left to our needs.

Now, when we enter the wilds, we go in with the best of camping equipment, with communications well established and the knowledge we can leave whenever we wish. No longer is it a question of endurance or survival. The element of fear has been eliminated, and now for the first time we can appreciate wilderness for what it is. To modern eyes the wild is a thrilling experience, beautiful to observe, fascinating to study.

But though the time has come when we can afford to be generous, when our understanding of the meaning of wilderness has changed, we still find it hard to change our traditional attitudes regarding it. The old pioneer concept of exploitation is still very much with us, the battle between bare hands and the forces of the wild not so easily forgotten. Though we may live in comfort, though the days of hardship and struggle are vague memories deep within us, still burn the old desires and fears. For that reason, many still feel that no place should remain inaccessible, that no resource no matter how small should remain unused, that the long battle for the possession of America will not be finished until the last square mile of wild country is crisscrossed with roads and telephone lines, every last acre under cultivation or management.

The prevalence of this pioneer tradition is the cause of the lethargy apparent when we are confronted with the loss of important wilderness areas. It is responsible for the battle waged constantly to preserve and hold the last tiny remnants of the America that was. Pioneers at heart, only a generation or two removed from the empire builders who spanned the continent with steel, the lumber barons who gutted the great timber stands, the hunters who decimated the buffalo, it is hard for us to change. Those days when the resources of America were thought inexhaustible, when all unbroken country was a challenge, are still very much a part of our consciousness. Inherently we are still a part of the great era of exploitation, insist on believing blindly the old myth of plenty. It is small wonder that the great majority finds it difficult to be concerned about the preservation of wilderness.

Its conservation becomes therefore a conflict between the relatively few who recognize its worth and those still enthralled by outmoded dreams of empire. These latter are the groups who clamor for roads into the last open spaces, who plead for dams across any river that is still wild and free, who present convincing arguments for harvesting the remaining stands of virgin timber within our last reserves. Because they often represent power, they have great funds to expend in accomplishing their aims. Legislators, always aware of the importance of their constituents, are easily moved by the possibilities of increased local revenues. Talk of esthetics and intangible values never seems to measure up to the concrete evidence of swollen payrolls in some isolated community benefiting directly by the exploitation of a hitherto forgotten corner of untouched country.

In spite of our traditional concept of the place of wilderness, there is, however, a growing recognition of its real worth. Many organizations are doing valiant work in educating the public. Our national agencies believing in the worthwhileness of wilderness preservation have already taken important steps to safeguard what is left. But even so there is much work to be done. We cannot afford to relax.

Perhaps the most encouraging development today is the wide interest in wilderness recreation and adventure. Canoe trips through the lakes and rivers of such areas as the Superior-Quetico country have become increasingly popular during the past decade. Pack trips through the mountains of the West as typified by the Trail Riders expeditions of the American Forestry

Association are indicative of the wide appeal of primitive experience. Hiking and mountaineering are playing an important role in the use of wilderness areas.

Americans are discovering again that living under primitive conditions is healthful fun, that what their forefathers did is not only good for their bodies but good for their souls. The need to escape the stress and strain of modern life is apparent everywhere. People feel they must re-establish their old contacts with the earth and simplicity, renew old perspectives, escape periodically from too much comfort and artificiality.

The medical world, viewing with alarm the tensions of our modern industrial civilization, sees in wilderness experience an opportunity to regain serenity and poise. Aware of the close affiliation between physiological well being and state of mind, it watches with satisfaction the swift return of bodily tone under the influence of wilderness living. Knowing the part the wild played in our development as a race, it is not hard to see that we need the very things we have left behind.

Important though such experience may be to physical welfare, its most valuable asset is without question in the realm of the spiritual. The very presence of wilderness is a balance wheel to civilization, a reminder of the basic problems of existence. The fact that here people can gain perspective and a sense of oneness with mountains, forests, and waters, enriches their lives, makes them better able to withstand the forces to which they must return. To countless thousands, wilderness has become a spiritual necessity.

People who feel deeply about the recreational possibilities of wilderness are willing to fight for its continuance. To them exploitation becomes anathema because they have known at first hand what it can mean to personal happiness. They are the groups who lend their support on every battle front where wilderness values are threatened. They are the first line of defense. While their numbers are still comparatively small, their voices are being heard, and the day may come when they will be strong enough to meet the challenge of those who still feel that here are the final opportunities for profit and personal enrichment.

Economically, wilderness is becoming an important resource to communities dependent for their existence on the development of recreational facilities. Though present in all such areas are individuals who are not aware of the real values involved, nevertheless, there is a growing appreciation of the fact that undeveloped country has tremendous appeal and significance, that it is always the magnet that makes people return.

The further we are removed from our primitive era of development, the more important these last reservations become from an educational standpoint. Such regions are living pictures of the America that was, the type of continent our forefathers knew. It is impossible to understand fully our social structure or our economy without recognizing the part of wilderness in its development. Here was opportunity as well as threat. It eliminated the weak, gave power and influence and often wealth to those strong enough to exploit it.

We are apt to forget the part it played in shaping our destiny as a nation. Those days already seem legendary. We think of the founders of our country in terms of the dim past, see no connection between what they did and the problems of today. We take all we have for granted, have become blasé and content, even critical of the ideals for which former generations fought and died. In order to understand, we must see the old backgrounds at first hand. Only then can we appreciate the present and evaluate the future intelligently. We cannot lose sight of our past without losing our perspective. It is good for us to have places which show us the road over which we have come.

Historical museums full of quaint and dusty exhibits often lack personal significance and identification. They seem removed from our lives. How different to travel down the lakes and portages of such an area as the Quetico-Superior country, knowing one is actually following the unchanged trail of the voyageurs, seeing the shorelines they saw 200 years ago. The realization that this was the America these intrepid adventurers knew when our civilization was but a thin line of struggling villages along the Atlantic seaboard gives meaning to their exploits and dreams. To camp where they camped, using the very same rocks for our fireplaces, to follow the ancient portages that felt the tread of their moccasined feet, to read the old diaries while listening to the sounds of the wild they knew, gives one a feeling for early America that can come in no other way.

To ride perhaps with a pack string down the primitive trails of the Rockies, knowing that this was the way Lewis and Clark and the mountain men knew the West, makes one share their experience. The peaks and breath-taking vistas are still the same, "The Shining Mountains," as bright as ever. But more important than all else is the feeling of remoteness and solitude that can still be found there. To live such a life even for a few days means a new appreciation of exploration, gives us faith in the purposes and ideals which drove these men to their goals. Somehow we get a new understanding of the meaning of courage and the vision which prompted these men to leave the comforts of established communities to fight their way across a wild and hostile continent to the Pacific. It gives dignity to the whole concept of democracy, makes us prouder of our heritage. To the youth of America this is a type of education beyond price.

Because we are the greatest race of earth movers in the history of mankind, the entire biotic picture is rapidly being changed. With tremendous ingenuity in the invention and manufacture of equipment, we are able to alter the courses of rivers, dam watersheds, and irrigate deserts at will. We build super highways across difficult terrain. Mountains and impassable bogs are no longer barriers to our advance. Our energy is inexhaustible. Where once we sought merely to subdue the wild, we now must rebuild it, revamp it to our needs. Our last remaining wild areas are threatened as never before by the same pioneer enthusiasm for conquering the forces of nature as guided our destinies in the past.

From the standpoint of science, this poses a real problem, for it is a major premise of research that there must be undisturbed areas for control purposes. Such areas are the norms, the common denominators for all investigations having to do with ecological adjustment. Without them, it becomes impossible to evaluate the significance of change. This is particularly true with regard to wildlife management. No program can be successful unless there is full knowledge of the traditional environment. Behavior patterns, set by countless centuries of adjustment to habitat, are the result of a vast multiplicity of influences. Animals do not swiftly change their habits or their physiological needs. They react as they do because of ancient backgrounds. It would be senseless to consider the wolf without understanding the extent or meaning of the old migration and hunting trails. No one could ever know the answers to the problems of deer propagation without taking into account not only their old food and breeding habits but also the relationship between them and the larger predators. Familiarity with life habits under primitive conditions is the key to all successful experimentation. Remove control areas, eliminate comparisons, and sound management becomes impossible.

What is true of animal ecology is also true of plants. Range and forestry problems arise from changes in the primitive environment, are usually an outgrowth of our failure to recognize the old relationships of types to climate and terrain. Check plots of original vegetation are necessary in order to know what is wrong. Diseased stands of timber must be compared with healthy primitive stands in order to determine cause. To the plant ecologist, control plots of undisturbed growth are as necessary to successful diagnosis and management as normal individuals to medicine. Only through knowledge of the normal is it ever possible to give a true evaluation of the abnormal or diseased. Scientific investigation based on the all important wilderness is therefore vital to our forest and agricultural economy. The productive power of America may be seriously hampered if opportunities for sound research are eliminated.

From the standpoint of economy alone, undeveloped areas are destined to play an important role. One cannot lose sight of the fact that even though our present reserves are relatively small they are the last untouched repositories of the great resources our continent once knew. As such they should be thought of as savings accounts for the future, as final untapped supplies of timber and wildlife, as guarantees that America will never be caught entirely short.

The fact that wilderness regions are recognized conservers of our dwindling water supply, that only through the presence of sufficient cover over the headwaters of our streams is it possible to prevent runoff and erosion, gives them enormous significance. Western irrigation projects would suffer indeed were such protective areas neglected. In order to maintain the lowering water tables in many areas, an extension of such forest cover is imperative today. Coupled with the fact that this would not only create new environments for wildlife, but would make available many important recreational regions to fill the growing need for wilderness experience, would indicate an expansion of our present wilderness area system.

In spite of the growing knowledge that undeveloped country is vitally important, we are still forced to fight a running battle for its preservation. Tied in with the old and ever prevalent concept of exploitation, there is also a very real threat in the private ownership of lands within the declared boundaries of most wilderness areas. Scattered through them are thousands of acres of land that our public agencies have not been able to acquire, with the limited funds at their disposal.

The Superior Roadless Areas along the Minnesota-Ontario border created to preserve the famous wilderness canoe routes of the Superior National Forest are typical. Within the million-odd acres of this reservation are scattered some 114,000 acres of privately owned land. Until the advent of commercial air transportation, these lands were kept from development by the roadless area restrictions, but now they are suddenly within a few minutes' flight from seaplane bases just beyond the borders. As a result, summer homes and resorts are swiftly changing the character of the canoe country. In spite of the fact that recent legislation has authorized half a million dollars for acquisition much harm has already been done. In many places failure to acquire private lands has practically nullified the very spirit and intent of the entire roadless area plan.

Many untouched regions in the United States face the same problem. Unless swift acquisition programs are invoked, and airspace reservations achieved to protect the wilderness, many superlative areas will be damaged beyond repair. The country itself might not change, but the spirit of the wilderness itself will be destroyed once solitude is violated.

There is a battle ahead on every last frontier. If we lose, America must bid goodbye to what has become a great spiritual and recreational resource. She must give up her living museums of the past, forget the role they play in scientific research. She must abandon forever the part of wilderness in her future economy.

It is time the American people became educated to the great values of our wilderness areas, and it is the duty of all conservationists to bring before the public the significance these areas have to national welfare. People should be shown the various ways in which they influence our wealth and happiness. We still have the opportunity of safeguarding what is left, but the time is short.

This is a challenge not only to the United States and Canada but to our neighbors to the south. The realization of our mistakes can be their opportunity, for where we have only three-fourths of one percent of our total land area set aside, many regions of Canada, Mexico, Central, and South America have still space and room to expand. By working together now and coordinating policies of land management and zoning, it may still be possible to set up a system of wilderness areas in the Western Hemisphere that would be a model to the rest of the world.

Living Wilderness, Autumn 1948

The Quetico-Superior Wilderness Laboratory

In this article, Sigurd advocates preserving the canoe country and other wilderness areas because of their great value to ecological research. Written for high school science teachers, this is Sigurd's only article focusing entirely on the scientific values of wilderness.

THE QUETICO-SUPERIOR FOREST extends for almost 200 miles along the international border from Lake Superior to Lake of the Woods. Once the route of the colorful and intrepid French voyageurs, fortunes in fur came down its beautiful waterways. Explorers traveled through it in their long search for the Northwest Passage. It has flown the flags of three nations and has been recorded in legend and history as one of the most unique and interesting regions of primitive lake country in the Middle West.

Today thousands of modern voyageurs explore it, paddle down the lakes traversed by the adventurers of the past, and pack over the ancient portages that once felt only the tread of moccasined feet. From the standpoint of recreation, historical significance, and economics, this area has become vitally important to the millions of the mid-continent. Here people not only breathe the spirit of the past but experience a scene that is practically unchanged from the days of discovery.

But there are others—the scientists and students of both the United States and Canada—who have found the area a fascinating place. Along the wild waterways of the Minnesota-Ontario border they have discovered opportunities for study and research in undisturbed forests, lakes, and bogs. One of the most interesting research projects of the last few years is the work of Dr. J. E. Potzger, an eminent paleobotanist of Butler University. Repeated borings of the peat bogs of the Quetico-Superior have enabled him to paint a picture of the past, the progression of the forests toward their climaxes, the cyclic successions of growth and decay.

According to Dr. Potzger, the many lakes of the region were formed by glacial action, gouging of the bed rock itself, the damming of streams by glacial debris, or by the melting of great chunks of moraine-covered ice. Peat bogs are lakes that have become filled by the accumulation of vegetation over the centuries. Once I looked through his microscope at sections of his peat borings, at pollen grains from 10 to 150 microns in size that were as sharply defined today as they were when they drifted into the lakes thousands of years before. He explained that they were composed of protein surrounded by an almost indestructible outer covering which seemed to defy the processes of decay; that even after long periods of time, it was possible to identify them.

The age of the material from the borings is determined by the radioactivity of the carbon deposits. Time and age can be measured in peat because of the known rate of decrease of the radioactivity of the carbon involved. Dr. Potzger estimated that it has taken from 500 to 1,000 years for a foot of such peat to be formed in the old lake bottoms of the Quetico-Superior and that several generations of forest may be recorded in a foot of any boring. Studies such as his are important for they afford an understanding not only of the past but of the present and future. To know what the actual successions have been gives an idea of what they might be in the future. Hitherto, records of forest growth have been scarce, but now we have a known and positive record running back thousands of years. Prediction becomes, therefore, no longer a matter of guesswork but of certainty not only in the Quetico-Superior area but wherever such research is possible.

This interesting work in the great wilderness laboratory along the border is only one of many research projects carried on today. Wildlife management, silviculture and forest management, the varied fields of botany, zoology, ornithology, entomology, and ichthyology are being continually explored. In all of these related fields it is becoming more and more evident that complete understanding depends on an undisturbed ecological setting for control purposes. This is a major premise of scientific research.

Wilderness areas are the norms, the common denominators for all investigations having to do with ecological adjustment. Without them it becomes difficult and often impossible to evaluate the significance of change.

With regard to wildlife management, this is particularly true. No program of management can be successful unless there is full knowledge of the traditional environment. Behavior patterns set by countless centuries of adjustment to habitat are the result of a vast multiplicity of influences. Animals do not change their habits or physiological needs swiftly. They react as they do because of ancient backgrounds. It would, for instance, be senseless to consider the wolf without understanding the meaning of the old migration and hunting trails. No one could ever know the answers to the problems of deer, moose, or caribou without taking into account not only their old food and breeding habits, but also the long and intricate relationship between them and their predators. Familiarity with life habits under primitive conditions is therefore the key to successful experimentation. Remove control areas, eliminate the opportunities for observation and comparison, and sound management becomes impossible.

What is true of animal ecology, is also true of plant ecology. Range and forestry problems arise from changes in the ancient environment and are usually an outgrowth of our failure to recognize the old relationships of types to climate and terrain. Check plots of original vegetation are necessary in order to know what is wrong. Diseased stands of timber must be compared with healthy primitive stands in order to determine cause. To the plant pathologist, control plots of undisturbed growth are as necessary to successful diagnosis and management as normal individuals are to the practice of medicine. Only through knowledge of the normal is it ever possible to give a true evaluation of the abnormal or the diseased. Scientific investigation based on the all-important wilderness is therefore vital to our forest economy. The productive power of America, leaning as it does on our forests, may be seriously impaired should opportunities for sound research on a broad and comprehensive scale be eliminated.

During the past 30 years, conservation groups on both sides of the international border have carried on a continuous effort to preserve the wilderness character of the Quetico-Superior Forest. First came the roads and the promoters who wanted to construct highways into all of the major lakes of the region; then waterpower development which, had it not been stopped, would have raised the levels of some of the lakes as high as 80 feet, destroying waterfalls, rapids, islands, and shorelines; after that, the effort to protect all shorelines from cutting; and finally, the invasion by the airplane which was settled by the now famous Air Space Reservation of the Roadless Areas of the Superior National Forest.

What conservation groups hope for now is that Canada and the United States will ultimately reach an international agreement as to broad conservation and land management principles which will protect the wilderness lake country by zoning while there is still time and guarantee the sanctity of shorelines, islands, and portages. Such an agreement would also insure sound forestry practices, wildlife, and resource management for the entire Quetico-Superior region on both sides of the border. Proponents of this plan recognize that the area, being a geographical unit, must have similarity of administrative policies in order to eliminate threats against it in the future.

In the face of our expanding population and industrial economy it becomes increasingly important to preserve wherever we can such wilderness areas as the Quetico-Superior. From the standpoint of ecological research large areas are necessary, for without distance and space, it becomes impossible to provide the buffer zones which are needed to protect inviolate wilderness interiors from foreign influences. While small regions may suffice for certain types of studies, for the broader biotic concepts there can be no substitute for extensive terrain. This is one of the important reasons for the preservation of this great wilderness laboratory.

How does this apply to the science students and teachers of America who do not have ready access to large and undisturbed regions for study but who, in practically every state, can reach parks, preserves, refuges, and similar natural areas for observation? The same general premise holds: that natural areas, no matter what their size, are nevertheless the controls, the norms in which it is possible to make studies and draw conclusions as to past conditions. All of them are valuable remnants of primitive America and should be cherished and protected, not only as museum pieces but as scientific research areas, for they are our links with the past, our indicators for the future.

Science Teacher, November 1951

Those Intangible Things

This talk, which Sigurd gave early in 1954 at the Izaak Walton League of America's national convention in Chicago, was his first attempt to discuss in detail the concept of "intangible values." It was a topic he came back to again and again, and in his later years he rewrote the speech for his 1976 book, Reflections from the North Country.

At the time Sigurd gave this talk he was the Izaak Walton League's fifty-five-year-old wilderness ecologist, and he was completing his first year as president of the National Parks Association. He also was just about ready to search for an agent for the book manuscript that would be published by Alfred A. Knopf two years later as The Singing Wilderness.

To TALK ABOUT THOSE INTANGIBLE THINGS is difficult because they are hard to define, explain, or measure. You can measure soil and you can measure water and trees, but it is very difficult to measure intangible values.

Before I begin to talk about intangible values, let us try to define, if we can, what they are. Intangible values are those which stir the emotions, that influence our happiness and contentment, values that make life worth living. They are all tied up with the idea of the good life. Sometimes I wonder if we actually know what the good life means. But this we know—that whatever it is, the intangible values are so important that without them life loses its meaning.

We talk about the practical considerations of conservation, and they are important, too. We know that we cannot embark on any conservation program entirely on theory. Back of all concrete considerations, however, are always other factors which we call the intangibles. They are what give substance to the practical; they provide the reasons for everything we do. Their values are so involved and integrated in all conservation work that it is impossible to separate them.

There is no question about the intangible values of works of art. We have always recognized them. I was over in the Art Institute yesterday morning and saw a woman standing engrossed before a great painting. She stood there in reverence, her head bowed. I looked at her closely and in her eyes was a strange, happy light.

What was she getting out of that picture? She was certainly not interpreting it in terms of the canvas that was there, the beautiful frame, or the amount of oil and pigment that artist had used. She was catching something which inspired her as it has inspired many others. She was enjoying the intangible values in that particular work of art. Ask her what it was she saw and she might not be able to tell you, but it did affect her deeply, and that was all that mattered.

Is it possible to explain the intangible values in a beautiful piece of music? As you listen perhaps to a Beethoven sonata, can you explain exactly what it does to you? There too are intangible values.

Do you know why you like a particular poem? What do William Cullen Bryant's lines do to you:

> Whither, 'midst falling dew
> While glow the heavens with the last steps of day.

What do those lines from "To a Waterfowl" do to you duck hunters? I know what they do to me. They are far more than

just words printed on a piece of paper. They embody sunsets
on the marshes, the whisper of wings, and many things that
others do not know. Bryant caught something in those lines,
something which you know and I know, the intangible values
of ducks against the sky.

There is no question in our minds of those values inherent
in works of art and I believe there is no question as to the intangibles involved in conservation.

There have been a great many definitions of conservation.
Aldo Leopold, whom you all know and revere, said, "Conservation means the development of an ecological conscience."
I am not going to try and explain fully what is meant by an
ecological conscience, for it would take a long time and there
are men sitting on either side of me who are probably much
better prepared to discuss that with you. But what I think he
meant was that unless man develops a feeling for his environment and understands it; unless he becomes at one with it
and realizes his stewardship; unless he appreciates all of the intangible values embraced in his environment, he does not and
cannot understand the basic need for conservation.

I think of [Louis] Bromfield's brief definition: "Conservation is living in harmony with the land." More simply, he was
saying what Leopold said. What is meant by "in harmony with
the land"? Certainly not the creation of dust storms, or gullies,
or mining the soil. In harmony with the land means living the
good life on the land.

I ran across a definition not long ago which points up particularly what I am trying to say. I like it, and I think you will
too, and I want you to remember it because it ties together all
the other definitions I know and gives substance to the idea of
intangible values. It was Paul Sears of Yale who said,
"Conservation is a point of view and involves the whole concept of freedom, dignity, and the American spirit."

A beautiful thing to say, and something that will be repeated for generations to come. Conservation is a point of view. It
is a philosophy and a way of life.

What do we mean by our way of life? How many of us know

what the good life is? Generations of Americans have enjoyed this thing we call the good life. In fact we have taken it for granted as part of our due without ever trying to define it or wonder where it came from. This much we know—that the good life is one of plenty, of breathing space and freedom, and for Americans it means the out of doors. If the open country was taken away from us and the kind of outdoors we know, would we still be living the good life?

Is our country heading toward a state of mechanized civilization where the good life as we understand it is going to disappear? Are we going to mistreat our natural resources to the point where it is no longer possible to enjoy the kind of good life we have imagined was ours forever?

I flew over the city of New York the other day. For some reason the plane circled over the miles and miles of tenements and slums that is Brooklyn. As we circled I looked down and wondered about the good life, thought of the children down there who never saw grass or trees or clean running water. I wondered what they thought about the good life and if they knew what it was?

I also saw Central Park that day, a little green oasis far below, surrounded by the roaring, bustling city of New York. That little natural area was worth uncounted millions of dollars, but then I knew its intangible values to the people of the city were far more important than any others. Here was a sanctuary of the spirit in the midst of one of the greatest industrialized cities of the world.

How is all of this involved with the conservation of our natural resources? What does it actually have to do with the practical problems of soil and water and living things? You have heard much about soil at this convention, and I am not going to enlarge on the subject. I merely want to quote Sterling North, who said, "Every time you see a dust cloud or a muddy stream, a field scoured by erosion or a channel choked with silt, you are witnessing the passing of American democracy." I would have added to that statement five words—"and our way of life."

More and more we are talking about the relationship of

natural resources and their conservation with our way of life. One of our great historians, in describing the migration of races from east to west, said, "In dust and rubble along those great migration lanes are the palaces, pyramids, and temples of the past."

Old civilizations can be traced along those lanes where man was on the search for food. What happened to those ancient peoples? They mistreated the land, their forests, and their waters, and thereby lost their way of life. They failed to recognize the intangibles before it was too late.

It is easier for me to think of the intangibles with respect to water than most other resources, for I've always lived close to it. When I say "water" I instinctively think of my own country, the Quetico-Superior and the wilderness canoe country of the international border. What is the importance of that country, its timber, its vast deposits of iron and other resources? There is no denying the part it plays in our economy, but when I think of it, I remember the vistas of wilderness waterways, the solitude and quiet, and the calling of the loons. They are the intangible values which someday in the future with our zooming population may far outshadow all others in importance.

Water. I think of Izaak Walton and the verse in the stained glass window of the cathedral at Winchester, England, where he is buried. There are only four words—"Study to be quiet"—but they embody his whole philosophy and way of life. Here was his search for tranquility and peace, here the whole reason for his communion with the out of doors. He did not mention the number of fish he caught. He remembered the quiet and the intangible values of the things he wrote about.

I visited Crater Lake, Oregon, this past summer and remember its startlingly blue water, its high peaks and snowfields. I remember especially how it looked in the early morning when it was half covered with mist. It is one of the most dramatic vistas on the continent and possibly in the world. Intangible values? Capture them? You bring them away with you but you cannot explain them.

I remember a little trout stream of a long time ago. I had

followed it to the headwaters on the advice of an Indian who had told me I would find a pool that no one had ever fished. I found that pool after looking for it for two whole days. I have never gone back there, and I do not want to go back, because I've heard that the pool has changed.

That pool was about the size of this room. There were great trees around it, primeval yellow birch, huge white pines and hemlocks. It was a rock pool, and I climbed out on a ledge and looked down into water that was clear and deep. Down on the bottom were schools of speckled trout, just laying there fanning their fins. I remember tossing a pine cone onto the surface and how the water exploded with rising trout. I sat on that ledge for a long time and watched those trout and all the great trees around the pool, and I thought to myself, "This is something very special; this is a part of America as it used to be."

Some years later, I described that pool in an article I wrote. "This," I said, "must be what we all think about when we sing, 'Thy rocks and rills, thy woods and templed hills.'" Here was something perfect. There were no dollar values around that pool, only intangibles.

Whenever I think of little rivers, I think of the 23rd Psalm, "He leadeth me beside still waters; He restoreth my soul." Again, the intangibles and spiritual values.

And what about wildlife and the intangibles there? Do you duck hunters remember how many ducks you shot last year or the year before? No, but you remember the sound of wings in the dawn or at dusk. You remember as though it was yesterday that mallard hen quacking far out in the rice and how the rushes looked when they were gold against the blue water.

One day just about eight years ago, I was walking along a river in Germany. It was quiet and dusk and there was a dull glow in the west. On both sides of the river were the silhouettes of bombed buildings, and a bridge lay broken in two in the current. I wasn't thinking of duck hunting, for it was spring and I was far from home, but then I heard a familiar sound, a whistle of wings overhead. I looked up and there was a flight of mallards heading down the river. For a moment I forgot everything and was back in the rice beds of the Minnesota lakes. The whistle of those wings were intangible values to me.

Last summer on a pack trip in the Sun River country of Montana we were riding through a dense stand of spruce in the bottom of a canyon. I got off my horse to lead it around a windfall and there in the center of the trail I saw the track of a grizzly. We never did see the bear, though we found where he had scratched great marks in the bark of a spruce as high as he could reach. From that moment on the country changed. It was the land of the mountain men of another century, the country of Lewis and Clark, part of the Old West. Those grizzly signs belonged to the intangibles.

It is hard to place a price tag on these things, on the sounds and smells and memories of the out of doors, on the countless things we have seen and loved. They are the dividends of the good life.

Have you ever stood in a stand of virgin timber where it is very quiet and the only sounds the twittering of the nuthatches and the kinglets way up in the tops? John Muir once said, "The sequoias belong to the solitudes and the millenniums." I was in the sequoias not long ago and it was a spiritual experience. To realize that those great trees were mature long before the continent was discovered, that their lives reached back to the beginnings of Western civilization, was sobering to short-lived man and his ambitions.

We need trees. We need them for our mills, for industry, for paper. We must have them for our particular kind of civilization. They are an important factor in our economy. But let us not forget that there are other values in trees besides the practical, values that may be more important in the long run.

You heard today that by 1970 there will be a fifth mouth to feed at every table of four. What is that going to do to our way of life? What is it going to do to the places where a man can still find silence and peace?

I read an editorial in the *New York Times* last year when the Supreme Court of the United States gave its favorable decision on the validity of the air space reservation over the Roadless Areas of the Superior National Forest in northern Minnesota. The heading of the editorial was "Tranquility Is Beyond Price." Tranquility is one of the intangibles. Solitude is also one of them. Those things are truly beyond price.

Much of my time is spent in the effort to preserve wilderness regions of the United States. They are the wild areas set aside by the states and the federal government as forests and parks. A constant effort is necessary to save them from exploitation. What we are fighting for is to preserve this less than one percent of our total land area. We are thinking of those places not only in terms of the physical resources within them but of their spiritual resources and intangible values.

The fact that last year forty-six million people visited our national parks and over thirty million our national forests, indicates that there is a hunger, a need in the American people to renew their associations with unspoiled nature.

We are trying—and when I say "we" I mean the Izaak Walton League together with all other conservation groups, the National Park Service, and the U.S. Forest Service—to hold the line and pass these areas on unimpaired to future generations, so that there will always be someplace where men can find peace and quiet.

And so when we talk about intangible values remember that they cannot be separated from the others. The conservation of waters, forests, soils, and wildlife are all involved with the conservation of the human spirit. The goal we all strive toward is happiness, contentment, the dignity of the individual, and the good life. This goal will elude us forever if we forget the importance of the intangibles.

Unpublished speech, 1954

Our Need of Breathing Space

During the first three months of 1958 Sigurd Olson was one of twenty-three prominent conservationists and scholars who spoke at a series of six panel discussions sponsored by Resources for the Future, Inc., and held at the Cosmos Club in Washington, D.C. The series was held in honor of the fiftieth anniversary of President Theodore Roosevelt's precedent-setting Governors' Conference to discuss natural resource problems. Each session started with a presentation by a major scholar, and then two or three other panel members took turns giving their own reactions at some length. The two-hour sessions included the opportunity for audience participation in the discussions. Later, the speakers edited their comments for inclusion in a book.

Sigurd was a member of a panel discussing the topic "Urban Growth and Natural Resources." The lead presentation, "The City's Challenge in Resource Use," was given by Luther Gulick, president of the Institute of Public Administration. Sigurd's talk was largely a reaction to Gulick's presentation, although he also took issue with a statement made by the famous economist John Kenneth Galbraith in one of the earlier panel sessions in the series.

Sigurd's talk is noteworthy in several respects. First, his tone is markedly more pessimistic than usual about the fate of postwar America. Second, it demonstrates more than any of his earlier talks and articles his concern that Americans need to preserve not only large areas of wilderness but plenty of smaller green spaces in and near the urban areas where most people live. Because of the lack of planning and control of development, he said, "urbanization in its present form is a threat not only to our economy but to our physical and spiritual welfare." Finally, regarding wilderness, he makes a telling comment, describing wilderness as a place "where there is no design, no planning whatsoever, no management of plants or animals, where people may sense what this planet was like before man achieved the power of revamping it for his needs." As the introduction to this book explains, this would be considered a radical viewpoint among wilderness supporters today, and yet it is supported by the implications of recent work in chaos theory.

❄ ❄ ❄

THE URBAN SPRAWL IS HERE TO STAY; it will continue and increase in the foreseeable future. Anyone who has flown over the United States during the past few years cannot help but be impressed with the evidence of this movement into the countryside. This growth is especially dramatic when flying at night, when cities and their radiating arteries of traffic look like skeins of Christmas tree lights, giant flowing tentacles reaching out into the dark, probing farther and farther into the surrounding land. There was a time not very long ago when you could leave the glow of metropolitan centers behind, but today, especially in the eastern half of the country, one barely leaves one glow before being conscious of another in the distance.

Nor is there any question but that this urban development exerts a great drain on natural resources. Luther Gulick has pointed out graphically what a high standard of living has done, what metropolitan services mean in terms of natural resources use, the attendant results in terms of air and water pollution, energy consumption, flood control, the use of the land itself and its ultimate removal from any use but that of real estate. It is in this respect particularly that I would like to supplement some of his ideas.

He states, "We will need more acres of open space within easy reach . . . totally new concepts of recreation . . . active programs for some, contemplative opportunities for many, and glimpses of beauty for all."

I could not agree more wholeheartedly, and I challenge anyone to contest the importance of these objectives. The great question, however, is how to reach them.

Dr. Gulick says further that ultimately urbanization will make possible the true conservation of the land. This is entirely possible, but with the type of uncontrolled and unplanned development now going on, it is highly improbable. We might come near to realizing the possibilities if we could regulate the nature and character of the extension of cities; if we could confine the growth within reasonable limits. But until we do, urbanization in its present form is a threat not only to our economy but to our physical and spiritual welfare. In the interim all we can hope for is to sandbag the flood wherever we can, hoping that eventually the high waters will subside of their own accord.

The inference that population growth will eventually be controlled by the attainment of an even higher material standard of living than we now enjoy, and a higher cultural level, and that through them population pressures may be brought into a far better ecological balance than most Malthusian predictions postulate, also seems doubtful to me. Certainly there is no sign in the postwar generation that a high standard of living is inducing social, political, and fundamental cultural attitudes that will bring about a better ecological adjustment.

Inasmuch as the dream of most urban dwellers is to get into the country, and industrial developments are moving out as well, this trend is bound to continue. The urge behind all of this is not new to Americans. We are a people who, until recently, lived close to the soil. Coming from pioneer and immigrant stock, many of us from farms and small towns, we have deep within us the feel of the frontier and the so-called "good old days," the feel of living and, if possible, working away from congestion and city sights and sounds and smells. While few urban dwellers would want to exchange their way of living for the past, there is a definite nostalgia, not only evidenced by the urban growth into the open country, but by the tremendous increase in recreational travel, the fifty-odd million going into our national parks annually, the demand for camping, hunting, and fishing opportunities.

Ask the average city dweller what he thinks is the ideal life, and what might contribute to his greater happiness, and he will no doubt think of possibly another car, a bigger TV screen, a longer vacation, and less traffic to contend with. Ask him if the American dream means the disappearance of little towns with shady streets, open countrysides, to be replaced by greater and greater industrialization with smoke stacks instead of trees, polluted air instead of the smells of fields and woods, gadgets and labor-saving devices replacing simplicity, with the feeling of the out-of-doors in his daily life becoming more and more a memory, and he will shrug his shoulders and wonder if you are slightly insane. Instead of the old music his forebears listened to, and the rhythms of nature and seasons which regulated their lives, he has listened so long to the drums of the Chambers of Commerce that the American dream has become synonymous with the goal of unlimited exploitation and economic growth.

While we have made great progress in developing knowledge of conservation during the past fifty years, we still are a long way from understanding and accepting Aldo Leopold's classic concept of an "ecological conscience," or as Dr. Gulick says, "an awareness on the part of urban man of his relationship to the world of nature."

I am not as sanguine as he as to what we can do about this. While it might be true, as Dr. Gulick suggests, that with our highly developed techniques of education and communication, "it should be possible to build a valid new idea into our fundamental culture within a generation or two," we all know that any educational program as broad and basic in its concepts as this, affecting as it ultimately must the entire basis of social planning as well as our mores, will take the kind of money, brains and organization, guidance and leadership that we now seem to be throwing into the arms race. Only with a similar sense of urgency, under dedicated and inspired leadership, can this be done. Only through education and subsequent government action can the problem be solved permanently. It will take an enormous effort and all the ingenuity we possess. The tragedy of the situation is that as yet there is no sense of urgency and no leadership that might bring about powerful governmental support and financing.

We are confronted with a situation where urban growth is so fast, changes coming so swiftly, that we cannot wait for the slow processes of education. New cities are mushrooming without any planning, great housing and industrial developments going on with no thought for breathing spaces, parks, or recreational needs generally. Already the need is being felt in suburbia, but still there is no design, no city or community planning, the result being confusion and subsequent loss of social values. In the city of Washington there is even serious consideration of sacrificing park areas for expressways. The bulldozers of big contractors, real estate operators, and industrial engineers are dictating the shape of cities of the future and the way a people must live. There is no thought of living "in the flow of nature." Urban man has thrown plans to the winds and is living a catch-as-catch-can existence dominated by impermanence, speed, and fluidity of movement. He is divorcing himself from the earth, and in this divorcement he is losing contact with elemental and spiritual things, his sense of oneness with his environment, psychological and physiological needs for which he has been conditioned for a million years by an entirely different existence. Ecological adjustments and adaptations take aeons of time. They do not take place in the short space of a few generations. Man is not yet ready for a capsule existence in a highly organized and artificial world, removed from the privilege of living close to the earth and experiencing the forces of nature and living in harmony with them.

It is wonderful to have national parks and forests to go to, but they are not enough. It is not enough to make a trip once a year or to see these places occasionally over a long week-end. We need to have places close at hand, breathing spaces in cities and towns, little plots of ground where things have not changed; green belts, oases among the piles of steel and stone. Children especially need this contact, for they have not as yet been weaned from the primal needs of the race. We need, in addition to such places, some areas large enough to be set aside as wilderness, where there is no design, no planning whatsoever, no management of plants or animals, where people may sense what this planet was like before man achieved the power of revamping it for his needs. Such regions, while they might seem to have no economic use, would act as buffers to a civilization that might destroy man's equilibrium and sanity. It is perhaps not without reason that Thoreau said, "In wildness is the preservation of the world."

In John Kenneth Galbraith's discussion of the economics of natural resources he implied that conservationists were so concerned with preserving isolated wilderness regions that they could not see the importance of controlling such blights as billboards along our highways. His statement indicated a lack of understanding of what conservation as a movement really means. While the control of billboards is a challenge to "Keeping America Beautiful," it cannot be considered in the same category with the broad aspects of soil, water, forests, and wildlife, the preservation of recreational areas, or unrenewable resources which can never be replaced—matters that have to do with the very basis of our culture and richness of living. While economics are important, it must be remembered that unless resources are preserved there will be nothing for economists to work with. With respect to urban developments, if planning does not now result in the setting aside of breathing spaces, planners of the future will be confronted with a frozen, crystallized situation where human needs can be satisfied only through enormous expense and physical difficulty.

Dr. Gulick says, "It may be found that a combination of

governmental, economic, and cultural institutions will lead to an adjustment of population to fit consumption and space use levels in conformity with the flow-of-nature policy."

Such a utopia is highly desired and I do not say it cannot be achieved, but in the light of our attitude, our preoccupation with material things, the character of our mushrooming civilization, it is highly improbable that it can come about early enough to save the situation before we are forced to face the problems that determined a way of life in the Middle East. There is no alternative today. We must move into this vacuum without all of the preliminaries of preparation, move swiftly with courage and vision, confident that the future will prove the wisdom of our action.

This is a difficult thing to do in a democratic system. We must stop talking about natural resources, recreational areas, and conservation generally in cold-blooded economic terms, seeing them only as graphs and statistics, national income and expenditures, taxes, price supports and programs. We must see them from an ecological point of view involved with such inherent needs as freedom, human dignity, and happiness. We must recognize the human necessity of keeping physical contact with the land, knowing now and in the generations to come the meaning of the old simplicities and satisfactions. While we may well be able to provide synthetics in fuel, food, and materials to take the place of exhausted resources of the past, cope with an expanding population without starvation or want, the great question will always be: Is this enough, is this the kind of a world we really want to live in?

Once having decided what we want and recognizing that there is no time to waste, no time to wait for the orderly and logical results of an educational program extending across decades, the question before us is: What can and what must be done now? The answer is first of all to find the leadership, and then for city, state, and federal governments to move immediately into the field of natural resources, doing everything possible to bring them into adjustment with consumption.

While there is still time, governments must also attempt to plan urban developments so that recreational areas of all kinds are set aside to meet the needs of a burgeoning population. It makes little difference what the immediate designations of such reservations may be. The important thing is to acquire and preserve them before they are gone forever. At the most, we have a decade to accomplish this purpose. If we wait much longer than that at the rate we are building now, the land will be gone and our opportunity for the future as well.

In Henry Jarrett, ed., *Perspectives on Conservation:*
Essays on America's Natural Resources
(Baltimore: Johns Hopkins, 1958)

Beauty Belongs to All

As a popular freelance writer for the leading outdoor magazines in the 1930s and 1940s, Sigurd Olson played an important role in building a steadily expanding tourist trade to the Quetico-Superior canoe country. Getting enough people to come to a wilderness area and fall in love with it was essential in building the political power necessary to preserve the area, but it also led to a decline in the very wildness that conservationists hoped to preserve. More people meant less solitude and silence, and, as Sigurd discovered, a surprising number of people thought nothing of cutting green trees for wood or shelter, or of leaving trash strewn at campsites and portages. The importance of beauty to the wilderness experience was not a new concept, but in the past the threats to beauty in the canoe country had been from logging and dams; in the postwar era the average visitor, simply because of growing numbers, became a new threat.

Sigurd first addressed the problem of proper wilderness behavior in an article called "Wilderness Manners," published by Sports Afield *in May 1945. He also reprinted it in pamphlet form to give to canoeists who used the services of the Border Lakes Outfitting Co. (He founded the company with two other men in 1929 and remained a partner in it until 1951, when he got out of the guiding business.) The problem continued to grow during the 1950s, however, and in 1959 Sigurd wrote about it again. He reworked "Wilderness Manners" for a national Canadian magazine,* Forest and Out-

doors, *and he wrote the following article for a Minnesota audience.*
"Beauty Belongs to All" is similar in style to the books for which he
had already become famous, and is the finest of these articles.

Note that acceptable wilderness behavior changes with the times.
Sigurd had cut tent poles in his early years, and used boughs for
mattresses, but in this article clearly disapproves of such behavior.
At the same time, he sees nothing wrong with sinking tin cans and
other garbage in the center of a lake, something that later would
become anathema to him and to the vast majority of canoeists.

❈ ❈ ❈

ALL DAY I HAD THOUGHT ABOUT the island campsite at
the north end of Robinson Lake in the Quetico. We had come
down the border from Basswood Lake, had portaged the brawling rapids of the river to Crooked Lake with its cliffs and Indian
paintings and were now threading our way up the Robinson
River. As we neared the outlet at the southwest end of the lake,
the campsite was more than ever in my thoughts for it was a
favorite of mine and one of the most charming in a country
noted for its beautiful campsites, the landing a smooth shelf
of glaciated granite, the fireplace close to the water's edge, the
tent site back in a fine stand of young red pines. It commanded
a breathtaking view of the narrows to the north and the full
sweep of open water to the south and in front across a narrow
channel were the cliffs and timbered ridges of Robinson peak.

A hundred feet along the shore was a spit of white sand extending out into the shallows. Sand pipers were always there and
gulls swooped low over their nesting rocks just beyond. This
enchanting spot seemed to combine all of the exquisite beauty
and poetry of the Quetico-Superior in one place.

I had been coming there for many years but each time was as
thrilling as the first. Never did I leave without being sure it was
as immaculate as when I came and always left some kindling for
the next party coming in, shreds of birch bark, a handful of dry
needles, some sticks to catch the blaze. And I was not alone in

my love for the island campsite on Robinson. Many others felt as I and though none of us had ever met we shared identical feelings and had an unwritten pact to keep it clean and unchanged. Some years before a family with three little girls had stopped there for several weeks. Before leaving they had taken a piece of birch bark from a down tree, inscribed it with their names and a plea that whoever came after them should also cherish the place they had found and take care of it. Some time later another family group had been there. They too inscribed their names and thanked the girls for what they had done, assuring them they felt the same. Over the years there were many contributors all sharing a sense of responsibility and companionship.

This was one of the reasons it was a joy for me to come there for I could almost feel the love and deep appreciation of all who had enjoyed it. Never did I find a can, a bit of string or tinfoil, or any cast off clothes. The fireplace was always thoroughly drenched and clean with that inevitable last word in courtesy, the little pile of kindling and wood. The tent poles were always stacked neatly against the lower branch of the same pine, the rocks and pegs left in an orderly pile.

Now I was close again with the same anticipation I had always known. No one would be there this time of year for it was late fall and the storms had begun, not long before the sleet and snow. The shores were still in full color, however, aspen and birch solid gold, the water as blue as it can only be in October. In a few protected places the maples still flamed and beneath the pines the blueberries were a mat of crimson. This was a day of peace and quiet, a fitting approach to the island campsite on Robinson Lake.

As I neared, however, I had a feeling that all was not well. A strange white spot showed clearly on the rocks of the landing, something that had never been there before. A big frame of poles stood where the tent used to be and there was a mound of something dark on the shelf of rock. Perhaps I thought, someone was there after all, but no movement could I see, no smoke, no overturned canoes.

As we swung in toward the landing, the spot of white took shape, a torn shirt draped over a bush and as the canoe drifted into its old berth bedside the ledge, my fears were realized. Down in the clear water were beer cans and other tins shining brightly against the bottom. Just off shore were fish cleanings, potato and onion peelings, and several sunken paper cartons. On the old log table was a pile of dirty rags and some discarded food and in a tiny moss lined pool a pair of socks.

We beached the canoe and walked up on the shelf. Between the fireplace and the water's edge, the lichen covered slope had been marred by a huge bonfire. Into this fire had gone logs and stumps and piles of pine branches. The fire had burned off mosses and lichens that had been accumulating there for centuries, had cracked off huge slabs of granite.

The fireplace had been changed, the blackened rocks had been rearranged to accommodate some type of cooking outfit different from the standard pots and pans of the usual canoe traveller. The tent site was the worst, for a huge rack of poles had been built up around it, and on top of the framework was a heavy thatch of balsam and red pine boughs. On the ground was just as thick a mat for a bed.

We stood there appalled at the destruction wondering why in this day of tents and airbeds anyone should have built such a shelter. In front of it a fire had burned deep in the duff next to a big pine and the flames had scorched the bark four feet above the ground. This was the place where our tent had snuggled cozily in an opening between the trees but that was hard to imagine now.

Sadly we walked down the trail to the beach and on the way found several tall white birches that had been peeled, the first time any of the stand had been mutilated. Hurrying on, I broke through the fringe of trees and stood on the beach. To my great relief, the sand was still clean and undefiled and there were the sandpipers tilting and running as always and the gulls swooping over their rocks.

Back at the campsite, we went to work for there was much to do before it would regain any semblance of its old order and cleanliness. In spite of all we could do, however, we realized it would never be quite the same again. The scar of the bonfire would remain for a century, the young pines and balsams that had been felled we would never see replaced in our lifetime.

We got into the water and fished out most of the cans and fish cleanings, went back and scoured the woods and came out with a poncho full of bottles and tins. Dumping the whole unsavory collection into the canoe, we paddled out a quarter of a mile where the water was at least a hundred feet deep and sunk it all being sure no cans floated away. The garbage and fish cleanings went the same way. In a short time aquatic life would consume everything and in time even the metal would be corroded completely by the chemical action of the water.

In rocky country such as the Quetico-Superior this is the solution to the disposal problem. To attempt to bury cans and offal is merely to invite flies, stench, and marauding bears. In deep water such garbage is lost forever and because of the great dilution there is not the danger of contamination there is in smaller and shallower lakes. The best solution of all is to carry no cans or bottles into the wilderness. With a great variety of excellent dehydrated foods now available, such weight is unnecessary.

The shirt, the old socks, the cardboard cartons, a pair of tennis shoes, and an assortment of odds and ends, we wrapped into a tight bundle, paddled over to a swampy bay, hiked inland until we found a deep hole in the muskeg, and pushed it out of sight down in the muck.

On our return, we rebuilt the fireplace, scraped out the ashes, some broken glass, and much charred wood, carried it back in the woods and buried it under a log. Then we took the cooking pails and washed off the place where the fire had been built until nothing was left but the bare rock.

For many years, ever since the air bed had been invented, balsams around campsites in the lake country had been relatively untouched, but this group had evidently read in some ancient book on woodcraft of the joys of sleeping on a bough bed and knowing nothing about air beds or the importance of not cutting trees on campsites had done the unforgiveable. For a few nights sleep, they had cut trees that had taken many years to grow, had either chopped them down or stripped them as high as they could reach with an axe.

Finally the old place began to look presentable again but it was late before we pitched our tent and cooked supper. After the dishes were washed, we walked over to the piece of birch bark still tied to the tree. The names were still legible, the message clear. We wondered as we stood there what the three little girls would think if they knew what had happened to their island. Perhaps by the time they returned most of the scars would be healed.

Many campers in the Quetico-Superior feel strongly enough about the canoe country not to violate it but there are always those without any background of experience or real love for the region who feel that because they are in the wilderness they have no responsibility, no reason to be careful of the places where they stop, or considerate of the enjoyment of others. These are the people who throw beer cans out of the windows of cars, who litter picnic and roadside stopping places with newspapers, cartons, bottles, and cans. They are the ones who dump their household garbage bedside the highways at night, who desecrate national parks and places of beauty everywhere. These we will always have with us for they have yet to learn that cleanliness is part of beauty and that beauty belongs to all. All we can do is set them an example, clean up after them, and somehow try to build up in the public consciousness enough appreciation so that the violation of any natural place is unthinkable.

We left the island campsite in the morning and continued to the north and in the course of our cruise found three more camps desecrated by the same group, the same littering of the camping area, the same unsightly structure of poles and pine boughs. Even the portages they crossed were defiled. They left a trail of ugliness in an enchanting wilderness and in so doing destroyed not only their own enjoyment but the pleasure of others who might follow.

Cleaning up a campsite, a lunch spot, or a portage takes little time, only a few moments to pick up the debris and get it out of sight. Every party should automatically look around before leaving to see that no sign whatever remains of their having been there. It is a small price to pay for the privilege of using it. If this could be routine procedure for all, there would be no problem for government cleanup crews or other travellers.

The lake country of the Quetico-Superior is without question one of the most delightful areas of its kind in the world. While there are many regions of lakes and rivers and forests, nowhere can be found such a combination of pleasing natural features as here, the gnarled red pines growing out of clefts in the rocks, the rugged little islands, the crystal clear water. Above and beyond its fishing, or the opportunity of traveling its historic waterways, is its unusual beauty. All who come must recognize their responsibility of leaving it as they found it. To do otherwise is to break faith with all for it belongs to everyone.

We talk about the intangible values of wilderness, but what is solitude made ugly through carelessness? A dirty campsite has lost its appeal, for cleanliness in this land of pure waters and rain washed rocks is swiftly destroyed. The federal and provincial agencies whose task is the protection and administration of this area do their best with limited funds and inadequate man-power but it is the users of the region who in the last analysis must do the job of preserving wilderness atmosphere. No agency, no matter how dedicated, can police and clean up an area so large and intricate.

Now with increasing use, the challenge is greater than ever before. Where a decade ago, there were only a few thousand using the region, now a hundred thousand enter it each season, canoeists cruising its interior, fishing and picnic groups from adjacent resorts, campers, hikers, and automobile travellers where its fringes are touched by roads. Among these are many who know nothing of wilderness manners or courtesy. This is to be expected for it takes time to get the feeling of a country.

Eventually, if they come often enough, they will develop an understanding of the significance of the Quetico-Superior and in time may begin to feel as all of us did about the little island campsite in the north end of Robinson Lake. When this happens as it inevitably will, then they will become as zealous in its protection as those who signed the birch bark manifesto on the island. This is the real hope for the future not only for this country but for all places of beauty wherever they might be. Where there is love and understanding, there can be no desecration.

Naturalist, Fall 1959

The Spiritual Aspects of Wilderness

The final major development in Sigurd Olson's thoughts about wilderness and the human spirit occurred during an intense period of reading at the dawn of the 1960s. Late in 1959, after completing a draft of his third book, The Lonely Land *(published in 1961), the sixty-year-old writer and conservation veteran thought he would write a book about his philosophy. "In Runes of the North," he wrote in an undated journal entry, "somehow must come in all of your mature reflections on life in general, what we are, where we are going, and why."*

To prepare himself, Sigurd read ten books between December 1959 and February 1960—works by Harrison Brown, Joseph Wood Krutch, Loren Eiseley, Lewis Mumford, Philip Wylie, Owen Barfield, Bertrand Russell, Julian Huxley, Pierre Lecomte du Noüy, and Pierre Teilhard de Chardin. He typed some sixty pages of quotes, paraphrases, and his own reflections. In the end, he did not use any of the material in Runes of the North, *which Knopf published in 1963, but he used it in speeches, in the final chapter of one of his 1969 books,* Open Horizons, *and in his 1976 book,* Reflections from the North Country.

It was during this period, while reading Julian Huxley's Religion Without Revelation, *that Sigurd first encountered the term "evolutionary humanism." And the books he read by Mumford, Lecomte du Noüy, and Teilhard de Chardin all agreed with the*

general idea: that humanity's destiny is to spiritualize the evolution-
ary process, leading evolution along the path toward an emergent
God. Concerned about the future of a world that was becoming
more materialistic and mechanistic, Sigurd believed that wilder-
ness could play a key role in helping humanity achieve its spiritual
destiny. The following speech, which he gave in April 1961 at the
Seventh Biennial Wilderness Conference, sponsored by the Sierra
Club and held in San Francisco, was Sigurd's first to show a glimpse
of his evolutionary humanism. He used parts of it in later articles
and speeches, in the final chapter of Open Horizons, *and in*
Reflections from the North Country.

❄ ❄ ❄

Henry david thoreau said many wise things, but
perhaps the wisest and most prophetic was his well known "In
Wildness is the preservation of the World." He said this over a
century ago during our pioneer era when the continent was still
uncrowded and largely undeveloped. Even then he could see
what was going to happen.

During the century since he made his far-reaching statement, we have opened up a Pandora's box of treasures. We
have discovered space-time, the atom, nuclear energy, and
probed the vastnesses of space. Evolution is an accepted fact
and we are swiftly unraveling the secrets of life itself and learning to synthesize what we need for survival on this shrinking
planet.

We are adopting a mechanistic attitude toward life in which
we believe science has all the answers, and are abandoning the
ancient verities and an appreciation of intangible values. We are
confusing mores with morals. We are embracing new beliefs,
philosophies, and nostrums which attempt to explain our relationship to the universe and to God. Our spiritual life is changing and as our roots are being cut, we attempt to substitute the
new ideas of the space age for the humanities and the intuitive
wisdom of the ages. As a result, within many of us is a sense of

insecurity, and a gnawing unrest that somehow the age of gadgetry and science cannot still.

A strange and violent world is ours, with the great silences replaced by the roar of jets and the cities we have built vibrating with noise. The smells of woods and fields and forests are now replaced by those of combustion and industry and our senses bombarded with impressions we have never known before. Were it not for a submerged racial consciousness steeped in a background that knew nothing of technology, we might make the adjustment more easily. Unfortunately, however, physiological and psychological adaptations take aeons of time.

"If we can imagine," as Richard Garrington said in his book, *A Guide to Earth History,* "that the entire four-billion-year history of the earth were compressed into a single year, then on this scale the first eight months would be completely without life. The following two months would be devoted to the most primitive of creatures, ranging from viruses and single-celled bacteria to jellyfish, while the mammals would not appear until the second week in December. Man as we know him would have strutted onto the scene about 11:45 P.M. on December 31st and the age of written history would have occupied little more than the last sixty seconds on the clock," and he might have added that the last century of the machine age would have occurred within the final second of the year.

Here perhaps is a clue to our predicament; the world has changed too swiftly for modern man so recently out of the primeval. He still moves to ancient rhythms, and his spiritual needs are the same. Though he is far removed from the past, it is not far enough for him to forget. Still part of his background, the song of the wilderness is clear and strong.

Not long ago I flew over the continent from east to west. As I left the Atlantic coast I pictured it as it was at the time of discovery, whales spouting off Nantucket, the timber tall and dark along the coastal flats, salmon and shad in rivers running clean and full to the sea, myriad wildfowl over the marshes. We crossed the fearsome Appalachians which for almost a century pinned

the first colonists to their beachhead. Deer and elk were everywhere then and it was said a squirrel could run clear to the Mississippi without touching the ground. We flew over New York
and Pennsylvania and were over the fertile valleys of the Midwest, then the plains where once roamed millions of buffalo, the
foothills, the gleaming Cascades, and then the dark line of timber along the coast of the Pacific, all in a matter of hours.

Our forefathers, I thought, had done rather well in four-
hundred years. Facing the unknown they had conquered a virgin
continent with their bare hands. To them the wilderness was a
power against which they pitted their own puny efforts, a condition with no compromise, something to be tamed and molded to their needs. This they must overcome or die. Waste was
of no moment, there was so much of everything; and so they
chopped and burned and made clearings, prospered and multiplied, and spread out toward the west. That frontier was one
of challenge and deep satisfaction. There was freedom and violence and adventure. Men lived and died with the light of adventure in their eyes.

The pioneer days are over and the entire complex of American life has changed. The land I saw that day is harnessed, with
roads everywhere, telephone, power, and oil lines enmeshing
more and more tightly the last remaining wild areas. It is a prosperous land and all the good things of life seem available for
those who want them badly enough. In spite of the tensions of
the cold war and the outbursts of fighting in many quarters of
the globe, there is optimism and hope. The next fifteen years,
say the financial wizards, will be the most dramatic in our history with an unprecedented population boom, an expanding
economy, and a national income beyond our wildest dreams.
With our inexhaustible energy we are not only subduing the
last of the primeval scene, but outside of a few protected areas
are shaping it to our needs.

Even half a century ago, most people lived close to the soil.
While cities were growing fast, the majority lived on farms and
in small communities not much different from the days of the

frontier. Though drastic changes were on the way, we were still not entirely removed from simplicity and naturalness. Then, spurred on by two major world conflicts, we were hurled into the whirring complexities of the machine age. We found ourselves cut off from any direct contact with the pioneer life we had known, discovered almost overnight we could live without having to hunt for food, carry wood or water, or even till the soil, that matters of security and community welfare were being taken care of by the state. After a long period of insecurity, danger, and fear, there seemed to be nothing more to worry about. Many believed the millennium had come.

In spite of all this, there was something missing, a sense of loss and incompleteness. While this experience was not unique to Americans, it was perhaps more poignant to them because of their own closeness to their recent frontier. The covered wagon days and the great migrations west were still near enough to be remembered. Men still lived who had seen the buffalo and the open range. The impact of the pioneer era was still very much alive though the physical evidence was largely gone from our lives. Though thrilled by our conquests of space, the detonations of jets breaking sound barriers, and the countless results of our inventive genius, we are now beginning to wonder if all this is leading to a fuller life.

In the days when our population was still around a hundred million, when airplanes were still in the barnstorming days, and our highways narrow gravel roads, when great areas were still unmapped, I was fortunate in being able to live in the wilderness. As a guide I traveled many thousands of miles in the Quetico-Superior country of the United States and Canada, living with all types of men under conditions which today seem almost as remote as the days of the Old West.

Even then, however, I was aware that something happened to men when they went into the bush. As they shed their city habits and settled down to the hard physical work and simplicity of primitive living, they laughed more and took pleasure in little things. Men who had not watched a sunset or a moonrise for years suddenly found such phenomena thrilling. They listened to the winds and the sounds of the forests and the roar of rapids lulled them to sleep. Men who had not looked at a flower, a bird, or a squirrel for a long time were not too busy any more for such simple pleasures. I once saw a business magnate engrossed for over an hour watching an ant hill, a man who until then had counted any moment lost that was not devoted to making money. Such things, I saw, became important as soon as men were removed from the complexities and responsibilities of the lives they had left.

I recall the strong loyalties and friendships developed on these expeditions, the feeling men had for each other and for the country itself, how they would plan from year to year and surround themselves in the meantime with mementos, maps, and relics from their trips, and count the days until they were heading into the bush once more.

And what did these men remember? Not the fishing, or the miles they had traveled, nor the game they had killed. What stayed with them was the good feeling after a day of tough portages or fighting some gale, the joy of warmth and food after exposure and reaching an objective under their own power. They remembered ghostly mornings when the mists were rolling out of the river mouths, days when the lakes were gay with whitecaps, evenings when the hermit thrushes sang and the west was flaming above the ridges. Theirs were visions of wilderness lakes when the islands lay like battleships before them, but most of all was the silence and the sense of removal. These were spiritual dividends, hard to explain, impossible to evaluate, that brought them back time and again. While they thought they came for the fishing or sheer adventure and companionship of such forays into the wilds, what they really came for was to experience the deep and abiding satisfactions of primitive living under natural conditions.

It was during those years that I discovered Thoreau and his belief that in wildness is the preservation of the world. While the idea intrigued me, it took a long time before I knew what

it meant. Not until I had spent many years traveling the bush
did the full impact of that truth strike home, that in wilderness
and all it entails in the broadest interpretation of the word is
the preservation of the human spirit.

During late years on expeditions into the North as far as the
Arctic coast and elsewhere, I have found that the magic formula
discovered long ago is still there, the joy and challenge of primitive travel, the sense of being part of a country and of an era that
is gone, the old freedoms, solitude, timelessness, and fullness
that always seems to come. As I watch my companions of today
I see the same reactions of long ago and as I think of Thoreau in
the light of what has happened, I know now that unless we preserve the kind of spiritual values to be found there and which
wilderness symbolizes, then man's future is bleak. The stakes
are high, the odds often overwhelming, but there is hope in a
people who have not forgotten their past and who at heart are
in love with America as it used to be.

In following Daniel Boone's Wilderness Road in the East,
the Trail of Coronado in the Southwest, the route of Lewis and
Clark, Alexander Mackenzie, Verendrye, and Samuel Hearne
in the West and North, I have recaptured a sense of history and
have seen the land through the eyes of those who saw it first.
How different Cumberland Gap looks when hiking through it,
and the Shining Mountains when riding a horse, how dramatic
lakes and rivers when seen from a canoe traveling a pace that
permits a country to sink into one's consciousness. This feeling
of identification with the terrain is a spiritual aspect that is
known at its best in wilderness. While it can be known almost
anywhere, to me it is a richer experience when it is removed
from towns and roads.

While I could not possibly know the fears the first explorers
knew, hostile Indians and the ever-present danger of ambush,
the loneliness away from those they loved, starvation and suf-
fering, and the dangers of penetrating terrain from which they
might never return, still I could sense the challenge, see the overwhelming expanses of land, and feel the silence. My apprecia-

tion was different from theirs for with me there was no uncertainty. I could enjoy it as they and the pioneers never could.
Seldom in their journals did they speak of the beauties of the
land they were traversing. Nevertheless that primeval land left
an impact on them that has given future generations strength
and fortitude and a longing to find again what once was part
of life on this continent.

Once long ago I met Jack Powell, half-Indian, living some
fifty miles from nowhere back in the canoe country. He had
been in for his winter supplies and was traveling alone, working his way slowly from lake to lake and over the portages.
I helped him over the last long carry on the Knife River and
then camped with him on an island down below. That night
we talked about the country and what might happen to it.
Even then when the area was practically unknown to campers
and canoeists, he had the feeling all frontiersmen get sooner
or later as civilization begins to move in.

"I'm going to get out of here," he said, "there are too many
people around. Why this spring after the ice went out, when I
was packing my fur in, there was some people on Knife I hadn't
seen before."

Many of us are Jack Powells underneath; and while there is
no longer any real frontier except in Alaska and the Canadian
Northwest, we show our restlessness by moving into the sub-
urbs or lacking that, by simply taking off for the wide open
spaces. All we want is a little room. The tragedy for those who
do move outside the metropolitan centers is to find that others
had the same idea and that secluded spots hewn out of the
woods are soon surrounded by a complex of superhighways
and shopping centers. The day may come when only on our
wilderness reservations will it be possible for moderns to experience what freedom of movement really means.

It is in the young that this urge is most alive. Each year they
embark on hazardous expeditions into the mountains, the
deserts, or the North with as little disregard for the consequences
as though they had lived a century ago. Just a year ago a group

of teen-agers followed the trail of Alexander Mackenzie through the Athabasca country and over a thousand miles down the great river bearing his name, ending at the Eskimo village of Aklavik on the Arctic coast. They suffered flies and mosquitoes, freezing water, and frigid gales off the Arctic ice, but they came through. Hungry to pit their strength and courage against the unknown, they returned with a new appreciation of their heritage and the hopes and dreams that had spurred their pioneer ancestors to fight their way across a hostile continent.

It is good to know that the old spirit of adventure is still very much alive in young America. As long as it is, there is little to fear. They think they go into the back country for a lark, just to test themselves, or to face a challenge, but what they really go in for is to experience at first hand the spiritual values of wilderness. They are going after them in the best possible way, traveling as Americans did a century or more ago. They will find the answers too, and what they find will nourish and sustain them for the rest of their lives. It may take years for them to realize what they found, but sooner or later it will come back to them, in a moment of stress perhaps, and when least expected, and then the almost forgotten memories of days in the wilds will give them strength and balance.

Thirty-five million of us bought hunting and fishing licenses last year and close to seventy million traveled to the national parks and forests. We take to the road, uncounted millions of us over week ends and holidays and for our annual vacations to the point where bumper-to-bumper traffic gives the impression that all America is on wheels. This going to the mountains, the lakes, and seashores, deserts, and plains is evidence of the need that lures young adventurers to climb mountains or head for the Canadian North. It is a nation-wide movement in search of things that seem to be missing in our present way of life. This is a character trait evidenced by a powerful desire, motivated by a hunger that only the out-of-doors can still, a distinct carry-over not only from our long primeval past but from a recent involvement with a frontier that accentuated what was latent within us.

We have only to look around us to see how much the past is with us. We build split-rail fences around our yards, have wells complete with sweeps and old oaken buckets, build artificial haycocks and shocks of corn, gather pewter mugs and plates to decorate the pine-paneled walls of rooms replete with hand-hewn, smoke-stained timbers. We watch *Laramie, Gunsmoke,* and *Wagon Train,* and our children play endless games of cowboys and Indians. On dude ranches throughout the West, we dress in chaps and sombreros and ride the range. In the Quetico-Superior, we are the voyageurs, freebooting fur traders following the lakes and rivers into the far Northwest.

Our love of exploration, pioneer settlement, and fantasy is genuine. We cherish every symbol and evidence that remains, and build them into our surroundings. A squirrel rifle over a fireplace mantle, wagon wheels at a gate, or even a starlit restaurant with guttering candles stuck in old green bottles, all evoke the past and keep our memories alive. While seemingly superficial, they have a strange power for they are mementos of a life that is gone. Like paintings or music or poetry, they represent intangible and spiritual values. If we have lost such things in our lives we try to bring them back by suggestion and inference. If they contribute even in the slightest something of what they mean, they are worthwhile.

In Montana just a year ago I saw an old, faded photograph of a buffalo hunt. In the foreground were several dead animals, the background was dotted with dark mounds as far as I could see. Two horses grazed quietly nearby. The killing was over and all that remained was to skin the carcasses and cut out the tongues. At the bottom of the picture was a painstaking scrawl of an old-timer who had sent this record of a bygone hunt to a partner, knowing the days of the open range were going forever:

To Joe: I am glad we was born when we was.
BILL

Millions of Americans today wish they had been born back then too. At least, comfortably ensconced before their TV sets, they *think* they would have liked it then, and would be willing to exchange comfort and security for danger and hardship if only they might taste a way of life that in retrospect seems rich and rewarding. We may seem blasé and materialistic, refusing to stand openly in support of the intangible values against the dollar values of exploitation, but underneath is a love and a need we cannot deny. The past still haunts our dreams. We hear the rumble of wagon trains, hear the war whoops of Indians, shiver with delight at the clatter of galloping hooves. All this is part of us and as long as it persists, latent and obscure though it may be, as long as we return to the wild places of our country of our own free will, or even dream about them, there is hope for us.

Should we ever forget and root out entirely any desire for wilderness, should we allow our engrossment with comfort and urban living and technological progress to completely erase our need for it, then I fear for America. A year ago at Portland I heard a speaker call a virgin stand of timber "cellulose cemeteries." I was so stunned I couldn't reply. But I didn't forget: "cellulose cemeteries." It shocked me and it hurt me. I lay awake nights wondering how to answer, and when your invitation to speak here came to me I said, "This is it."

I say now that if the time should ever come when Americans look at their last stands of virgin timber as cellulose cemeteries, if the time should come when they lose the intangible meanings of these forests—Muir said of the sequoias, remember, that they belong to the millennia—if that time should ever come, then I would say Americans have lost their battle.

But I do not believe this will ever come to pass, for I have faith in Americans, in their inherent love of their recent frontier, in their built-in reverence for beauty and the natural scene, and above all in their constant hunger for it. The very fact that you are here today indicates that there is hope for the future, that there is a growing realization among Americans of the intangible or spiritual values of wild country.

The real significance of wilderness is a cultural matter. It is far more than hunting, fishing, hiking, camping, or canoeing; it has to do with the human spirit. And what we are trying to conserve is not scenery as much as the human spirit itself.

Not only has wilderness been a force in molding our character as a people but its influence continues, and will, if we are wise enough to preserve it on this continent, be a stabilizing power as well as a spiritual reserve for the future. The intangible values of wilderness are what really matter, the opportunity of knowing again what simplicity really means, the importance of the natural and the sense of oneness with the earth that inevitably comes within it. These are spiritual values. They, in the last analysis, are the reasons for its preservation. This is what people seek when they go to the out-of-doors, the reason for the nostalgia and longing, not only of Americans but of all peoples who have divorced themselves from their backgrounds.

We are entering a new era in our thinking regarding wilderness. The fact that so many of us are gathered here today to discuss the cultural values of wild country is indicative of our growing comprehension of its relationship to our happiness. All over the land there seems to be an awakening in the public consciousness, as witness the articles, editorials, and books that have to do with the importance of its preservation. We are at last beginning to look at our remnants of wilderness with the maturity of a people who can see beyond purely economic factors.

Bertrand Russell said recently that "Wisdom is the harmony of knowledge, will, and feeling and we must not court cleverness at the cost of understanding."

"It is possible," he continued, "to live in so large a world that the vexations of daily life come to feel trivial and the purposes which stir our deeper emotions take on something of the immensity of our cosmic contemplations." If mankind can acquire this kind of wisdom, our new powers over nature offer a prospect of happiness and well being such as men have never experienced before.

I think Bertrand Russell put his finger on what it is that we are all trying to do. We are trying to bridge the gap between our old racial wisdom, our old primeval consciousness, the old verities, and the strange, conflicting ideologies and beliefs of the new era of technology. One of the most vital tasks of modern man is to bridge this gap. Though we as Americans cherish the frontier and all it represents, though we pride ourselves on our pioneer background, still there is uncertainty and even fear as to the future. None of us is naïve enough to want to give up what technology has brought or to evade the challenges now before us. This too is a frontier, not only of the mind but of the physical world. Somehow we must make the adjustment and bring both ways of life together. If man can do this, if he can span past and present, then he can face the future with confidence.

It is here that wilderness will play its greatest role, offering this age a familiar base for explorations of the soul and the universe itself. By affording opportunities for the contemplation of beauty and naturalness as well as further understanding of the mysteries of life in an ecologically stable environment, it will inculcate reverence and love and show the way to a humanism in which man becomes at last an understanding and appreciative partner with nature in the long evolution of mind and spirit.

Wilderness which once was home to all mankind is a vantage point where landmarks are known. Like one who is lost, a man can look about him and see where to go. There are many trails to follow but this one is sure. It is a way we have always known for here we are closer to the sources of that deeper intuitive knowledge and wisdom the race has always used as a guide during times of stress and confusion.

Cultural maturity comes slowly and the old conflicts between materialism and the intangible values will flame on many battle fronts for years to come. When the time arrives that we look at wilderness, not as savages, not as pioneer exploiters, but through

the eyes of enlightened man with understanding and appreciation of its real meaning, then and only then will the full measure
of Thoreau's statement be realized, that "in Wildness is the
preservation of the World."

In David Brower, ed., *Wilderness: America's Living Heritage*
(San Francisco: Sierra Club, 1961)

The Wilderness Concept

This article, published in an annual Iowa State University forestry department magazine, breaks no new ground for Sigurd. Indeed, quite a bit of it is cribbed from earlier work dating back to his 1946 article "We Need Wilderness." There are some additions and different phrasings, but the most interesting section is the final half dozen or so paragraphs. The ending, in particular, reflects Sigurd's deep concern for the fate of the world in 1962, the year of the Cuban missile crisis. The values and perspective needed to avoid nuclear war, he says, are an inherent part of the wilderness experience.

THE CONCEPT OF WILDERNESS PRESERVATION is new to Americans. Recently emerged from a frontier period where the goal was to subdue and eliminate primeval country to make room for farms and communities, it is difficult to suddenly look at wilderness as something to be cherished. Now we have reached a stage of cultural maturity where for the first time in our history we can understand its intangible values and the part they play in our lives.

The preservation of sample plots of unchanged nature, rocks and trees, lakes, rivers, and mountains, and all forms of life indigenous to them are only the outward manifestations of their

real significance. What they actually mean in an age where technological advance has outstripped humanitarian needs is to serve
as a spiritual resource.

Man has been on this planet for perhaps a million years having arrived through the slow tortuous processes of evolution
some four billion years after the earth was formed. If we were to
compress this tremendous time span into one year, man would
then be only fifteen minutes of age.

But only during the last 100,000 years, or less than two
minutes of this time, has he emerged from the primitive and
assumed the stature both physically and mentally of the Homo
sapiens we know today. And only during the last 15,000 to
20,000 years has there been any real evidence of cultural advance. During these ten to twenty seconds of his history he
built the ancient civilizations of the Near East.

Even a hundred years ago, three seconds from today, he lived
close to the earth and though civilization was changing swiftly, it
was still predominately agrarian with a pattern of life that with
few exceptions was one with the slow rhythms of nature.

Then around the turn of the century, we experienced the first
explosions of technological advance. Two great wars added im-
petus and urgency to scientific research and suddenly we found
ourselves literally hurled into the whirring complexities of an
industrial age. During the final second of man's span of life on
this earth, we have unravelled the secrets of the universe and
now are probing space itself.

It is a strange exciting world for man so recently removed
from natural things and he is convinced the millennium is at
hand. Cut off in a largely urban way of life from direct contact
with the earth, for the first time in his long primeval history,
he can live without having to hunt food or protect himself,
with matters of security and welfare taken care of by a benefi-
cial government. No longer does there seem anything to fear
except his own ingenuity in evolving engines of destruction.

In spite of comforts and diversions and a standard of living
higher than the world has ever known, evidence is appearing

that all is not well. There is wide unrest, frustration, and even boredom with the new life. The fact is that modern man in spite of his seeming urbanity and sophistication may not be ready for his new way of living, that physiologically and psychologically he is still so close to the simplicities and elemental struggles from which he so recently evolved that he cannot forget and that the old fears as well as the basic satisfactions are still very much a part of him.

Even though he is embracing new religious beliefs, new philosophies, and nostrums which attempt to explain his relationship to the universe and to God, there is a sense of incompleteness. Within him is a powerful nostalgia, he cannot understand, a gnawing unrest that the new world of gadgetry, and amusement cannot still. He dashes from place to place filling his leisure time with diversions, never daring to be alone with his thoughts. The old sense of belonging is gone and the inherent need of being part of a stabilized ecological complex. In spite of comforts and almost complete control of his environment, he is confused and insecure.

A strange and violent world is his with the great silences replaced by the roar of jets and the cities he has built vibrating with noise. The smells of woods and fields and forests are replaced by those of combustion and industry, and his senses are bombarded with impressions he has never known before. He has come a long way during the past 100,000 years and were it not for the submerged nine tenths of his subconscious, a subconscious steeped in a racial experience that knew nothing of technology, he might make his adjustment more easily. But unfortunately the biological and mental processes of any species refuse to be hurried. Adaptations take aeons of time.

G. M. Trevelyan once said, "We are literally children of the earth and removed from her our spirit withers and runs to various forms of insanity. Unless we can refresh ourselves at least by intermittent contact with nature we grow awry."

The great historian was right. We are literally children of the earth. When modern man steps into a dimly lighted cocktail lounge for a meeting with his fellows, he is back in his cave; when he checks the thermostat of his apartment, he is still kindling a fire; when he steps out on the street at night and sees Orion glowing in the sky even though it is dimmed by the lights of the city, he is doing what men have done since the dawn of the race. Man of the atomic age and its conflicting ideologies is still part of the past.

Such thoughts were much in my mind not long ago when I flew across the North American continent from the Atlantic to the Pacific. As I soared high above the earth, I pictured the country as it was at the time of discovery, whales spouting off Nantucket, the timber tall and dark along the coastal flats, salmon and shad in rivers running clean and full to the sea, the fearsome Appalachians that pinned the first colonists down to their beachhead for over a century. Deer and elk were everywhere then and wildfowl darkened the sky and on the western plains the thundering buffalo herds numbered millions. I flew across the dark and bloody ground of Kentucky and thought of the Wilderness Road, crossed the gleaming Mississippi then the vast plains and foothills of the Rockies and was over the Pacific in a matter of hours.

The colonists had done well. Facing the unknown they had conquered a virgin continent. To them the wilderness was a threat, a power against which they must pit their own puny efforts, a condition with no compromise, something to be tamed and molded to their needs. There was only one problem then, to eliminate the wilderness or die and so they chopped and burned and made clearings for farms and villages, built roads and towns, prospered and multiplied, and spread out toward the west.

This was work for which they were prepared and in spite of great hardships, the frontier to them was one of challenge and deep satisfaction. One has only to sing the songs of those days to know that life was full and rewarding. There was freedom and violence and adventure and men lived and died with the light of far horizons in their eyes. What they did not realize was that in the very process of subduing the continent, they were destroying conditions which gave them character, moral sense, and spiritual strength, all of which they would need in abundance in the years to come.

The pioneer days are over and the entire complex of American life has changed. The land is harnessed now, roads everywhere, telephone and power and oil lines enmeshing more and more tightly the last wild areas. Only in a few places is there any wilderness left in the mountains or the deserts or in such forgotten corners of lake and river country as the Quetico-Superior up along the Minnesota-Ontario border. The rest is tamed and subject to the will of man and all this taken place in the short space of four hundred and fifty years and most of it actually within the last century.

It is a prosperous land and all the good things of life seem available for everyone. In spite of the tensions of the cold war and the outbursts of violence in many quarters of the globe, there is optimism and hope. Business is expanding and the national income growing by leaps and bounds. Housing and industrial expansion are swiftly filling in the blank spaces between the towns. The face of the earth is being changed and with tremendous ingenuity in the invention and manufacture of earth moving equipment, we are turning loose fleets of gigantic behemoths which are altering the course of rivers, building super highways across terrain that until now was considered impassable. Even in the far north, huge wheeled tractor trains are plowing across the ancient tundras to the very shores of the Arctic Sea. With inexhaustible energy we are not only subduing the last of the wilderness but actually reshaping it to our needs.

As I looked down at the conquered land that day, I wondered how far we would finally go in its subjection, if our goal of unlimited exploitation of natural resources and expansion of our industrial complex would eventually destroy every last vestige of the old America, if our booming population would increase to the point where standing room is at a premium and the old freedoms and satisfactions are gone forever.

No one knows the answers to these questions. It is not easy for a people who are only a few generations removed from the frontier to change the pattern of their thinking swiftly. Millions still refuse to believe that resources are not inexhaustible and the frontiers a thing of the past. Inherently Americans are still part of the boom days with the exploitation of all resources and elimination of the wild the expected course of events. Talk of spiritual values still does not take equal place with the concrete evidence of an expanding economy.

While it might seem that our young nation has never thought seriously about the preservation of wilderness, even as long as a century ago, there was a stirring in many minds and a questioning of the wisdom of our headlong destruction of the natural scene. James Fenimore Cooper prophesied in his novel *The Prairie*: "When the Yankee choppers have cut their path from the Atlantic to the Pacific, they will turn in their tracks like a fox that doubles and then the rank smell of their footsteps will show them the madness of their waste."

The Yankees of the frontier no doubt laughed at Cooper and dismissed him as a visionary, but there were some who believed that what he spoke was the truth. Evidence of the vision of those who believed that conservation of natural resources and the preservation of wilderness was worthwhile was the setting aside during the last quarter of the 19TH century of such preserves as Yellowstone National Park, Yosemite, and Sequoia, the rest of the 31 national parks and 85 monuments that now comprise the present National Park System. Though less than one per cent of our total land area, it was a beginning. We also established during this period the national forests and eventually set aside within them 83 areas which now include some fourteen and one-half million acres classified as wilderness. Wildlife refuges, state, county, and city parks and forests were set aside to meet the need. Canada established its system of national and provincial parks even though her remaining wilderness resource far exceeded ours. It was an encouraging development and a tribute to those with the foresight to envision the future.

However, since these reservations were made they have been

challenged and weighed in the light of the old pioneer philosophy that has dominated thought on the North American continent since the days of discovery. Today we are forced to justify them constantly to protect them from industrial exploitation or commercial developments which could destroy them. During the past few years, we have fought invasion of the national parks, national forests, and wildlife refuge systems. Canada has lost to a great hydro-electric development one of its most magnificent areas in the west, Tweedsmuir Provincial Park.

The battles go on constantly and are increasing in intensity. The great task today of all interested in the preservation of natural areas is to justify them in the eyes of a people the majority of whom are still convinced that nothing should interfere with the grinding progress of our mechanical age. Even though many areas have congressional sanction and are seemingly protected by law and administrative decrees, it has become necessary to justify their protection from every conceivable angle.

Scientists know, for instance, that no program of forestry, wildlife, or soil management can be successful without full knowledge of an unchanged and traditional environment. It is recognized that behavior patterns set by ecological adjustment, interrelationships, and physiological needs can only be studied properly under undisturbed conditions. Plant ecologists point out that range and cover problems arising out of changes in the primitive ecology need control and check plots for proper evaluation of results. For identical reasons, agriculture needs virgin soil for comparisons. Wild areas are vital to all successful research and management and even to the layman such conclusions are valid.

Another argument is the educational value of such areas not only from the scientific point of view, but from the perspective of a history rapidly fading into legendry. It is important to recapture and hold the past, and the wilderness regions of the continent are being seen in the light of living historical museums. Our peers are showing the part the wild played in the development of our social structure and our economy and stress the importance of saving these areas so that we might glimpse the past and see the road over which we have come.

How much more satisfying to travel down the lakes and portages with canoe and pack over the routes of the French voyageurs than to read of their exploits in the dusty volumes of some library; how thrilling to ride the mountain trails of the Rockies and see the Old West as the explorers and wagon trains had seen it. This was good for young and old for it not only gave them the rare privilege of primitive experience but a new appreciation of their heritage and the courage and dreams that had prompted the pioneers to leave the comforts of civilization to fight their way across a hostile continent.

Wilderness regions are museums of nature in which all life and geological processes are still unchanged. America, used to the museums tradition and having spent millions on the housing and protection of works of art as well as the reconstruction of historical buildings, understands this aspect of preservation. How much more worthy of protection, say the advocates of wilderness, are the works of the creator which have come down to their present state only through the evolution and perfecting processes of adaptation. Here they point out is something to really cherish and protect, exhibits so wonderful that all other museums seem unimportant by comparison, here an opportunity to see the handiwork of God.

But it is the scenery of such areas that draws the millions. Magnificent scenery needs no explanation or justification and the fact that last year some fifty million people, almost a third of the population of the United States, visited the national parks and monuments was convincing proof of their appeal to the mass mind.

So to place a precise value on wilderness is as difficult as to place a dollar sign on the worth of an heirloom or a landmark. There are certain things that cannot be evaluated because of their emotional impact. Wilderness is in this category. While certain areas might have worth as a museum piece or because of certain scenic, scientific, or economic factors, its real worth will always depend on how people feel about it and what it does to them. If it contributes to spiritual welfare, if it gives them perspective and a sense of oneness with mountains, forests, and waters, or in any way enriches their lives, then the area is beyond price.

Some can find their wilderness in tiny hidden corners where through accident or design man has saved just a breath of the primeval. I know a glen in the heart of a great city, a tiny roaring canyon where many seeking solitude and beauty can find release.

But there are also those who crave action and distance and far horizons. No little sanctuaries for them along the fringes of civilization! They must know wild country and all that goes with it, the bite of a tump line on the portages, the desperate battling against waves on stormy lakes. They must know hunger and thirst and privation and the companionship of men on the outtrails of the world. When after days of paddling and pacing, they find themselves on some bare glaciated point a hundred miles from town and stand there gazing down some great waterway, listening to the loons and seeing the islands floating in the sunset, they know the meaning of communion.

Others find their wilderness in the mountains. There camped in some high alpine meadow with the horses grazing quietly along an ice fed glacial stream and all about them the grandeur of the snow capped peaks of some mighty range, they find their particular ultimate. To them such a setting is the primitive on a noble scale, there a timelessness than cannot be approached anywhere else. The very bigness of the landscape gives them contact with immensity and space. They come down from the hills as men have always done since the beginning time, refreshed spiritually and ready once more for the complexities of life among their kind.

There are those who say that only in the great swamps and flowages of the Deep South can one understand what wilderness really is. And in a sense they are right for it was in such places that life evolved. Some men sense instinctively that there conditions approximate the primeval and that a man gets a closer feeling with the past than in any wilderness.

The criticism that only a small minority of the population ever has such intimate physical contact with the wilderness way of life is relatively unimportant. While travelling by canoe, or with packhorses, or on foot may be the ideal way to experience wild country, the fact remains that the very existence of such areas has an enriching effect not only on adjacent terrain, but on all who glimpse them or are even aware that they exist at all.

Stephen Leacock when asked why he persisted in living in Toronto instead of returning to his beloved England, replied that he liked Canada because he was so close to the wilderness of Hudson Bay and that even though he never put foot in a canoe, the very thought of the thousands of miles of barren country to the north gave him a sense of expansiveness of soul that made life richer. In that statement he voiced the feeling of thousands who like him, though they never penetrate the wilderness, nevertheless are conscious of its presence and power.

Because wilderness means different things to people, when the final summary of values is made, the answer will no doubt be a combination of them all. But as yet there is no clear conception or acceptance of what it really means, no concrete understanding of why its preservation is a cultural necessity. If there was, there would be no pressures to exploit their natural resources or to convert the last great sanctuaries into amusements resorts. Only among those who have actually experienced the wild on expeditions into the interiors is there any real conviction of their worth. These people know for they have been shown and there is no doubting in their minds. But until all the people somehow catch their vision and understand its meaning, no natural area, no matter what its designation will long survive on the North American continent.

Whatever their type or wherever they are found, lakes, deserts, swamps, forests, or mountains they fill a vital need today as a spiritual backlog to the high speed mechanical world in which we live. Is it surprising when production lines and synthetic pleasures fail to satisfy the ancient needs of modern man that he instinctively turns toward the wilderness to find the naturalness and stability the race once knew? The eighty million who visited the national parks and forests last year thought they went for the scenery and the joy of travel, but what they really went for was to catch a hint of the primeval, a sense of the old majesty and mystery of the unknown. A mere glimpse of the wild set in motion dormant reactions long associated with solitude. The fifty million found that out.

A year ago, Justice William O. Douglas of the United States Supreme Court when on his famous trek down the Potomac River to call attention to the wilderness values of the valley, said: "We establish sanctuaries for ducks and deer. Isn't it time we set aside a few sanctuaries for men?"

While it is doubtful if our primitive ancestors knew much of the appreciation of the intangible qualities of their environments, we moderns do have that capacity and powers of perception that make it possible to appreciate the qualities of the earth that gave rise to those creative efforts that lifted man gradually from the dark abyss of the primitive to a state where he was able to express his deepest emotions of awe, wonderment, and religious belief in stone and color and finally in words and music. The wilderness concept has to do with the preservation of these wellsprings of the spirit for men of the industrial age.

John Galsworthy said it well:

> It is the contemplation of beautiful visions which has slowly generation by generation lifted man to his present state. . . . Nothing in the world but the love of beauty in its broad sense stands between man and the full and reckless exercise of his competitive greed.

In the development of the concept we must ask ourselves what sort of culture we want and whether or not we care enough about the old values to make the sacrifices necessary to preserve them. R. S. Baker said recently in an editorial in *Health*: "The greatest danger lies within ourselves, for who shall preserve wilderness when we lose our very desire for it. If we allow the hurly-burly of modern life to obscure our deep-seated need for wilderness experience, if we act like a race of spiritual dwarfs, the loss will be a great one indeed."

It behooves all nations therefore, and while there is still time, to look long and searchingly at their last wilderness regions before they abandon them to the maws of industry. In the United States, in Canada, Africa, South America, and Asia, wherever there are still areas of the wild, there is a great opportunity. We must not fail in our engrossment with physical needs to also make provision in equal proportion for the satisfaction of cultural needs. Any nation which today has the vision to set aside sanctuaries of the spirit for the swiftly growing populations of the future is acting in accordance with man's profoundest requirements.

In the days to come, the wilderness concept must be clear and shining enough to capture imaginations. It must take its place as a cultural force with all expression of man's deepest yearnings and his noblest achievements in the realm of the mind. It must be powerful enough to withstand everywhere in the world, the coming and enormous pressures of industry and population.

No greater decision faces mankind today, for in the choices that must be made may lie the future of the race and the road man must follow. If we should lose the very desire for those values that are inherent in wilderness and abandon ourselves to the mechanical robot age of automation, then the holocaust of atomic war might be the end of the long dreams of man and his endless search for beauty and meaning in the universe.

The Ames Forester, 1962

The Spiritual Need

*This is one of Sigurd's best speeches about the spiritual values of
wilderness; he gave it at the Ninth Wilderness Conference, held
in San Francisco in April 1965. This particular speech shows the
influence on Sigurd of one of the most important and widely read
Thomistic philosophers of the twentieth century, Josef Pieper.
Sigurd had bought and read Pieper's book* Leisure: The Basis of
Culture, *and the book clearly impressed him. Not only is Sigurd's
paperback copy full of underlined passages, but Pieper's words and
ideas about the spiritual aspects of leisure creep into this speech
and, later, into* Open Horizons *and* Reflections from the North
Country. *Sigurd's strong ending to the speech is in fact a partially
reworded version of* Leisure'*s opening epigraph, in which Pieper
wrote, "Unless we regain the art of silence and insight, the ability
for nonactivity, unless we substitute true leisure for our hectic
amusements, we will destroy our culture and ourselves." Sigurd
also mistakenly attributes to Thomas Aquinas a statement Pieper
made about "the landscape of the universe" during Pieper's discussion of Aquinas.*

I AM HAPPY TO TALK ABOUT the spiritual values of wilderness because I feel they are all important—the real reason for all the practical things we must do to save wilderness. In the last analysis it is the spiritual values we are really fighting to preserve.

Not all look to the wilderness for spiritual sustenance. Some seem to get along very well without it, finding their values in different ways. Others must know wilderness at first hand, must experience it physically, as well as spiritually. There is a great diversity in wilderness appreciation and wilderness need, but I have discovered in a lifetime of traveling in primitive regions, a lifetime of seeing people living in the wilderness and using it, that there is a hard core of wilderness need in everyone, a core that makes its spiritual values a basic human necessity. There is no hiding it. The core is there, no matter how sophisticated, blasé, and urbane one might be. Deep down inside all of us is a need of wilderness.

I shall not attempt to enter the vast realm of religious belief or the concept of a Deity, though there is a close correlation between them and the spiritual values of wilderness which in themselves are only one facet of the entire complex, a facet which cannot be disregarded in probing the problem of man's relationship to God and the universe.

In order to speak intelligently about such intangibles as the spiritual, we must attempt to define them, for they are often misunderstood and impossible to measure by ordinary standards. We are accustomed to associate the spiritual with such immortal lines as, "He leadeth me beside still waters; He annointeth my soul"; or "I lift up mine eyes to the hills from whence cometh my help." No one needs to explain or define the meaning of such expressions, for we sense intuitively and from long association and personal experience the joy and lift of spirit they epitomize. Even those who think wilderness means nothing share in this reaction to visions that actually had their origin in the ancient concept of far horizons, beauty, and silence.

There is far more, however, to the spiritual values of wilderness than the beautiful music of the Psalms and the emotional release they bring. Webster, in defining the spiritual, speaks of the soul, the essence, eternal values as opposed to the worldly or carnal—the imponderables as against the tangibles. A philosophy is involved, a way of looking at life, and a perspective that goes deeply into value judgments that affect our happiness.

We might argue any of these points and try to explain or analyze, as many have done before us. Volumes have been written by theologians and philosophers on their meaning, but the more exhaustively we delve into the discussions, the more we are convinced that argument is futile in view of the differences in individual understanding and belief stemming from reactions that range from the faintest glimmerings in comprehension to the ultimate beatific vision of the saints and prophets.

On one point all agree: that spiritual values contribute to joy and richness of living; that without them existence lacks color and warmth, and the soul itself is drab and impoverished. We accept the broad premise that such values, inspired by the contemplation of wilderness beauty and mystery, were the well springs of our dawning culture and the first significant expressions of the human mind. True in the nebulous past, it is as true today no matter how life has changed or what has happened to our environment.

I am confident that Stone Age man, who some forty thousand years ago painted his symbols on the caves of France and Spain, was powerfully stirred by the mystery of the unknown and the spirit world that dwelt there. Such surviving examples of prehistoric art tell of the millennia when man pondered his environment as an awareness finally dawned that the dreams, longings, fears, and hopes that haunted him could be translated into forms of meaning and permanence. Symbols from which spells and magic went forth to influence hunting, fertility, and success in his various ventures—they represented the growing world of the spirit, the first indications of the mighty concept of immortality, and the realization that after death men would dwell forever in the vast vault of the heavens. It was then he emerged from the dark abyss of his past into a world of mind and soul and began to give form to his deepest and most profound emotions.

But why, we ask, does modern man, now almost completely removed from his wilderness background, still look to the hills for his spiritual help in meeting the tensions and pressures of this age? Why does he yearn for open space and naturalness, for the sea with its immensities, for vistas across valleys and mountain ranges? Why on weekends and holidays does he stream from his crowded and clamorous cities into the open countryside?

Anthropologically, the answer is simple. A hundred thousand years have elapsed since man's emergence from the primitive, perhaps a million or more if we go back to the very beginnings of the race to which he belongs. During all this time he lived close to the earth, regulating his life by the seasons, hunting his food, knowing the fears, challenges, and satisfactions of a life entirely dependent upon nature. Only during the last forty thousand years did he develop any sort of culture and not until ten thousand years ago leave any evidence of historical record. Until the last century the broad pattern of his life had actually varied little. To be sure, there were cities long before that, but the vast majority of people lived on the land or in small rural communities still close to the influences of the past. Then in the space of a few decades, he was literally hurled into a machine age of whirring speed and complexity where the ancient ecological and emotional balances were upset and his way of life utterly changed.

In the light of his primitive conditioning, man is still part of the past, responsive to and dependent upon the type of environment from which he came. Adaptations come slowly in all creatures and man is no exception. When weary and confused by the life he is now leading, it is no wonder he longs to escape from the barriers he has built around himself. It is natural for him to dream of freedom and to look backward to a time when life was simpler, to old familiar trails where the terrain is known. There seems to be an almost universal urge, no matter what the stage of man's sophistication or removal from the natural, to align himself somehow with those forces and influences that were dominant for ages.

Stanley Diamond said: "The longing for a primitive mode of existence is no mere fantasy or sentiment whim; it is consonant with fundamental human needs. . . . The search for the primitive is as old as civilization. It is the search for the utopia of the past projected into the future; it is paradise lost and paradise regained . . . inseparable from the vision of civilization."

A man may not really know why he climbs a mountain, crosses a desert, travels by canoe down some strange waterway, or sees the national parks or the wilderness areas of the national forests from the comfort of an automobile. Somehow in spite of himself, the spiritual penetrates his consciousness, and he absorbs a sense of vastness, far horizons, and silence plus other intangibles always found away from cities and towns. It may not be realized until afterward, but in some moment of quiet remembering, the essence of wildness comes to him like an almost forgotten dream—the inevitable aftermath, the spiritual values responsible for the glow and the inner satisfactions such experiences leave.

Man's great problem today is to make the transition, to bridge the gap between the old world and the new, to understand the reason for his discontent with things as they are, and to recognize the solution. His old world of superstition, evil spirits, and fear is gone. Gone too his dependence on the wilderness and his sense of close relationship, belonging, and animal oneness with the earth and the life around him. He must recognize now that while some of his spiritual roots have been severed, he still has his gods, and that his attitude toward wilderness has entered a new phase in which for the first time in his evolution as a thinking, perceptive creature, he can look at it with understanding and appreciation of its deeper meanings, knowing that within its borders may be the answer to his longing for naturalness. He needs to know that the spiritual values that once sustained him are still there in the timelessness and majestic rhythms of those parts of the world he has not ravished.

With this realization, wilderness assumes new and great significance. It concerns all of humanity and has philosophical implications that give breadth to the mind and nourish the spirit. Because man's subconscious is steeped in the primitive, looking to the wilderness actually means a coming home to him, a moving into ancient grooves of human and prehuman experience. So powerful is the impact of returning that whether a man realizes it or not, reactions are automatically set in motion that bring in their train an uplift of the spirit. It is as though, tormented by some inner and seemingly unsolvable problem, he is suddenly released from frustration and perplexity and sees his way.

One of the great challenges confronting those who believe in the preservation of wilderness is to build a broader base of values than physical recreation, a base of sufficient depth and solidity to counter the charge that it exists for only a privileged and hardy few. Should this be possible, and I believe it is through stressing its all-encompassing humanitarian values, then there will no longer be any question of its importance to mankind. Only when the true significance of wilderness is fully understood will it be safe from those who would despoil it.

Josef Pieper, a German philosopher, in speaking of the meaning of leisure, said it is a form of silence, a receptive and contemplative attitude of mind and soul, and a capacity for steeping oneself in the whole of creation. He might just as well have been explaining man's attitude in approaching the wilderness.

He quotes Plato, who said: "But the gods, taking pity on mankind born to work, laid down a succession of recurring feasts to restore them from their fatigue so that nourishing themselves in festive companionship with the gods, they should again stand upright and erect."

Companionship with the gods and true leisure—this is perhaps what modern man seeks when he goes to the wilderness. This much we know is true: that while a man is with his gods, no matter who they may be, he can forget the problems and petty distractions of the workaday world and reach out to spiritual realizations that renew him. Only through receptiveness, contemplation, and awareness does anyone open himself to the great intuitions and consciousness of what life and the universe really mean.

Thomas Aquinas once said: "To know the universal essence of things is to reach a point of view from which the whole of being and all existing things become visible; and at the same time the spiritual outpost so reached enables man to look at the landscape of the universe."

I like the idea of looking at the landscape of the universe, for it condenses into one shining vision the whole concept of spiritual experience. By "essence" Aquinas means the reality of man's relationship to the universe of which he is a part. If a man can sense this, if he can even glimpse the infinity Aquinas talks about, he might see the landscape of the universe.

Some years ago, I accompanied the famous geologist and geographer Wallace Atwood on a glaciological survey of the Quetico-Superior country. We wanted to see what had happened to the old pre-glacial stream patterns of the rivers which ages ago carried the wreckage of the awesome Laurentian Mountains toward the seas of the south.

We sat before our fire one night and talked about what we had seen, but mostly we admired the beautiful specimens of porphyry we had found on Lake Saganaga. Dr. Atwood had a prize specimen in his hand, and as he turned it over and over, allowing the firelight to strike its crystals, his eyes shone.

"Tell me," I said finally, "how is it that near the age of eighty you still get as much pleasure and excitement out of finding a new specimen as though you were a geology student on his first field trip?"

He gazed in the fire awhile before answering. "The secret," he said, "is never to lose the power of wonder. If you keep that alive, you stay young forever. If you lose it, you die."

I have never forgotten what he said, and I know now that the power of wonder is back of all creative thought and effort, and without it scientists, artists, and thinkers in all disciplines would lose the spur and challenge to learn and explore the mysteries about them. Wonder becomes then a spiritual value, the basic source of energy and inspiration in the evolution of the mind of man. Though we may produce life and eventually know the answers to all the secrets, we must never forget that wonder was responsible.

Albert Einstein reaffirmed this truth when he said: "The most beautiful experience we can have is the mysterious. It is the fundamental emotion which stands at the cradle of true art and true science. I am satisfied with the mystery of the eternity of life and of being able, through awareness of glimpsing the marvelous structure of the existing world together with the devoted striving, to comprehend a portion of it, be it ever so tiny, of the Reason that manifests itself in nature."

Over the centuries a host of other great minds have also believed that if through awareness and wonder man might recognize even faintly his personal relationship to the universe, he would then partake and become part of the order and reason that governs his existence, the movement of galaxies, as well as the minutest divisions of matter. From the early scriptures and through all cultures, this profound concept has echoed and re-echoed as man realized its immensity and spiritual connotations. A grand concept, it has increased the stature of man and stood the test of time.

Prerequisite to understanding the lofty ideas of Plato and Aquinas is developing the capacity of awareness and wonder. If this ability is one of the important potentials of man, and the quality of inciting it one of the spiritual values of wilderness, here is an opportunity—for only by encouraging wonder in others and explaining to millions of people its true meaning, can we ever be sure of preserving any wilderness on our planet.

When Aquinas, in speaking of wonder, said, "Man's first experience with it sets his feet on the ladder that may lead to beatific vision," he meant what to him and other seers was the supreme climax of spiritual revelation.

The late Pierre Teilhard de Chardin, one of the loftiest minds of this age, in speaking of such moments said: "But now the atmosphere around him becomes sustaining, consistent and warm. As he awakens to a sense of universal unification, a wave of new life penetrates to the fiber and marrow of the least of his undertakings and the least of his desires. Everything glows as if impregnated with the essential flavor of the absolute, showing our accession beyond all ideologies and systems to a different and higher sphere, a new spiritual dimension."

While it is good to know how great minds feel and to bask in the aura of their perception, we realize we are ordinary men who must, in order to understand, translate such experiences into concepts that can be applied to the problems of living in an age seemingly dedicated to the destruction of ancient values and our environment. What can we deduce from their expressions that bear on the kind of wilderness experience we are concerned with? Is there anything tangible we can apply to life as we know it? What broad conclusions from their flights into mystery and revelation can we use? They speak of oneness and unity with life and the universe, of the eternal essence, and the perception of reality. What exactly does this mean to us?

Lewis Mumford gave us a clue when he said, "Man's biological survival is actually involved in cosmic processes, and he prospers best when some sense of cosmic purpose attends his daily activities."

Wilderness offers this sense of cosmic purpose if we can open our hearts and minds to its possibilities. It may come in such moments of revelation as Aquinas, Chardin, and others speak about, burning instants of truth when everything stands clear. It may come as a slow realization after long periods of waiting. Whenever it comes, life is suddenly illumined, beautiful, and transcendent, and we are filled with awe and deep happiness. All of us have known such moments but seldom recognized them at the time or comprehended their meaning. At least so it is with me and possibly with most of us whose experiences have come to us in the wilds.

I remember several such moments—an evening when I had

climbed to the summit of Robinson Peak in the Quetico to watch the sunset: the flaming ball trembling on the very edge of a far ridge—fluid, alive, pulsating. As I watched it sink slowly into the dusk, it seemed to me I could actually feel the earth turning away from it, and sense its rotation.

Once many years ago, I stood gazing down a wilderness waterway with a fleet of rocky islands floating in the distance. The loons were calling, echoes rolling back from the shores and from unknown lakes across the ridges until the dusk seemed alive with their music. I was aware then of a fusion with the country, an overwhelming sense of completion in which all my hopes and experiences seemed concentrated in the moment before me.

I shall not attempt to analyze my reactions nor correlate them with order or reason, and I believe to try would be a mistake. I was not particularly aware of destiny or my role in the great plan. What I did carry away with me was a sense of wonder and deep contentment, a certain feeling of wholeness and fulfillment as though I needed nothing more. It would take a greater and more perceptive mind than mine to explain their full significance, and were they to do so, they might discover our moments of revelation were the same.

Life as it is lived for most people today is a fragmentary sort of thing, and man often feels as impermanent and transitory as the things he has built. If through such experiences as these he can somehow catch a feeling of wholeness or a hint of cosmic consciousness, he will know what the sages have been trying to tell us. No two people have the same type of experience, nor do they ever come in identical ways or similar situations. When I think of man's spiritual need of wilderness, I believe that the opportunity of being aware of and knowing such moments is an important part of it.

If, as Harrison Brown said, "The spiritual resources of man are the critical resources," then wilderness, which fosters such values, must be preserved. If we can believe what the wise have said for thousands of years, then there is hope for wildness and beauty in our environment. If spirit is a power and a force that spells the difference between richness of living and sterility, then we know what we must do. It may well be that with our swiftly expanding population, the movement away from nature into vast city complexes and the decimation facing much of the land, that the wilderness we can hold now will become the final bastions of the spirit of man. Unless we can preserve places where the endless spiritual needs of man can be fulfilled and nourished, we will destroy our culture and ourselves.

In Bruce M. Kilgore, ed., *Wilderness in a Changing World*
(San Francisco: Sierra Club, 1966)

Remarks to National Park Service
Master Plan Team Members

*Sigurd Olson developed a close relationship with National Park
Service leaders after World War II, first as director of the National
Parks Association, and later as a member of the Park Service's advisory board and as a paid consultant to two different Park Service
directors. He served on several teams that prepared master plans for
managing national parks, and traveled the United States scouting
out potential additions to the national park system. He played a role
in the establishment of a number of national parks, monuments,
and other protected areas, from Cape Cod in the East, to Voyageurs
National Park in the Midwest, to Padre Island in the South, to
Point Reyes in the West. Over the years he traveled to Alaska many
times and was a member of the Park Service's Alaska Task Force,
which in 1965 recommended withdrawing roughly seventy-six million acres of outstanding wildlands in thirty-nine locations spread
across the state. Fifteen years later, these recommendations formed
the core of the Alaska National Interest Lands Conservation Act,
which was signed by President Jimmy Carter and protected one
hundred and four million acres, more than a quarter of the state.*

*Sigurd became a beloved figure among rank-and-file Park
Service employees, too, in part because of his tremendous effective-
ness as a conservation leader, but most of all because of their exposure to him at Park Service conferences. He frequently spoke at
these events, and while his messages often challenged Park Service*

employees to rise to meet some threat or opportunity, he also in-spired them and gave them a sense of hope that they could meet his challenge.

The following talk, given to National Park Master Plan team members sometime in the mid-1960s, shows not only his belief in the importance of wilderness to the national parks, but his talent for encouraging people to hold fast to their ideals in the face of sometimes strong opposition. The four-page transcript from which this comes appears to have been taken from a conference proceed-ings document put out by the Park Service, but only the portion containing Sigurd's comments is in his collected papers, so the original source is unknown.

❄ ❄ ❄

CHAIRMAN DAN BEARD: Our next speaker, who really needs no introduction, is a writer, an educator, philosopher, explorer, outdoorsman, canoeist, voyager, conservationist, and special consultant to the Secretary of the Interior—our dear friend, Sig Olson.

SIGURD OLSON: Thank you, Dan, for that rapid-fire résumé of impossible accomplishments. I won't even try to live up to them.

Sometime after the new Director [George Hartzog] came in, he and I had an early morning talk. We talked about the wilderness. I must have been rather inspired, because George said, "Can you put this into a caption, a brief statement that I can use, possibly with some of the Master Plans?"

I said, "I will try, George." But I never did. It is still on my desk marked "Urgent." Someday I am going to try to put down some of the ideas I discussed with George that morning. A cou-ple of the ideas stand out and those I will try to give you now.

We have heard a great deal about wilderness. The previous speakers on this program talked about it, and other program people have talked about it. The last few years, there has been so much talk about wilderness that we have become sort of

drifting or swimming in a flow of words, and I wonder sometimes if we aren't forgetting the real essence of what we are
talking about. We become so engrossed in our language, our
definitions, and our objectives that it is hard to say what you
really want to do or what you really want to understand in the
application of management plans or their development.

When a speaker gets up, he must have a few convictions,
otherwise pronouncements are not particularly valuable. I have
convictions; one is that the preservation of wilderness in the
National Park System is probably the most important management activity of the men in whose care these values are entrusted. I know you have all been concerned with the preservation
of wilderness. In the Master Plans that are coming up, you know
what you have got to do. In every individual plan, the same,
broad regional considerations Ted and Howard were talking
about yesterday give it even more impact. The preservation of
wilderness is vital and important because without wilderness,
park areas, historic areas, recreational areas, any type of area you
happen to think about or will be entrusted with, will lose its
essence, its atmosphere, its feeling. Without the preservation of
wilderness, particularly in our National Parks, beautiful scenes,
beautiful areas lose their significance.

I sometimes think that if the wilderness atmosphere were
wiped out, any scene, though still beautiful, would be merely
a façade of what it could be—sort of a window dressing. But
with wilderness, all scenes, no matter what their categories, assume much deeper and far-reaching spiritual significance.

The National Parks, I feel, have an overriding purpose,
and that can be encompassed in one word—*spiritual.* Spiritual values are values that affect your emotions, that affect
your happiness, that affect your culture. They are hard to
define, hard to pinpoint, but they are there. The National
Parks may look like pleasuring grounds, places for picnics,
overnight camps, places for taking pictures, entertainments
of various kinds, but no matter how you look at it, it is the
spiritual value of the National Park that the visitor carries

with him. Atmosphere and feeling apply to areas of prime importance.

One of the reasons that they are of such prime importance is that man of today needs escape. He lives in the jet age, the industrial age, the space age, an age of automation, growing technology, urbanization. The time is coming when the bulk of us will be living in cities, not little towns and farms, but cities. All these factors set up a hunger in people to escape for a little while and return to the natural, the primitive scene. They can do this in National Park areas. They can do this wherever they go to feast their souls on scenery and to catch this elusive something called "primitive."

This morning at breakfast, we were talking about wilderness and someone mentioned that it is difficult, or will be increasingly difficult to hold wilderness, in view of the fact that only a small percentage of the people actually go into it and use it. Two percent, three percent, or five percent will probably cover them all. That the vast majority of the people coming in don't pack, don't hike, don't sleep on the ground, but get their enjoyment or feeling of wilderness from the seat of an automobile or from an overlook looking across a primitive valley.

I think one of the most important things we can remember regarding wilderness is that everybody comes to a National Park to sense this wilderness we are trying to preserve, and the man looking at it from the seat of his automobile or from an overlook is getting, in a sense, the same kind of experience that he would get if he hiked in with a pack on his back. I belong to the packers. I like to do things that way, but we are in a minority group, and we have got to admit that we probably always will be. The automobile is wedded to the American way of life, and Americans are not going to walk, if they can ride. So, when we talk about wilderness preservation, just remember that we are not talking about a minority; we are talking about a hundred percent of the American people who come into these areas. It is for the vast majority, as well as the minority, that we are preserving wilderness. It is to keep the essence of the wild so that others can enjoy it.

One of the problems of the National Park Service is to preserve the integrity of these areas. We are all familiar with the old mandate. We are also familiar with the anachronism of trying to preserve wilderness in the face of increasing use, increasing population. It is a difficult situation. The National Park Service can be proud of what it has done, because it has had a conviction, too, running back a long, long time. How otherwise could the National Parks still claim that from 90 to 95 percent of their areas are still wild, still unchanged, unless there had been a definite depth of feeling guiding all of the pioneers? Of course, mistakes have been made, and attempts have been made to right them. Mistakes will always be made; sometimes they can't be righted. Sometimes they become irrevocable, and that is why management problems must be so carefully thought out with respect to wilderness.

Oftentimes there is no turning back. Oftentimes there is no second chance. But the Park Service has a sacred trust. In a sense, the Service is the guardian of part of the American culture—a culture deep in our frontiers, a culture of freedom, conquering the wilderness—which has become part of our minds and spirit.

Any attempt to preserve the primitive, to give people a chance to get their feet on the ground again and understand what reality really means, as opposed to the artificial and the changeable, is a good mission. Giving people the chance to get the feeling that they have taken hold of ancient verities is what we are trying to do.

What this Service is faced with now, more than any other time in its history, is a sense of urgency. Population is pyramiding to the point of saturation. Industry is speeding over the land. Super highways, power lines, oil lines enmesh the whole continent. And we hear the voice of change so loud and so clear that we cannot ignore it. Ribbon cities spreading out from the metropolitan centers connect with the other metropolitan centers. Never before has the Service faced such a challenge. It makes it all the more paramount that we entrench and try our best to hold the line and protect these areas that we have set aside.

America needs wisdom more than cleverness. We are clever people. Our inventive genius knows no bounds. We are changing the face of the earth, changing it entirely. Two great threats today are population and what we can do and are doing to cure it. There is one hazard that park people must be aware of and that is the danger of "tolerance." You can look at your area and say to yourself, "Something has got to give." So you give with a new road or a new facility or a new development. Something has got to give, and you follow through. You develop a dangerous tolerance.

I would like to leave this final thought with you. No matter what you are called, no matter what political pressures are brought to bear on you every time a new development is proposed, look at it carefully and don't be too tolerant. Give in, if you have to, but only as a last resort. What you have is a sacred trust, a trust that future generations will hold you accountable for. Let's not look ahead just the next ten years with a definite use graph. Let's give it the broad long vision. Let's think of a hundred years, five hundred years, a thousand years, and with all of the planning that you do, do not be shortsighted. Do not lean toward immediacy. Look ahead and plan for the future. Look ahead to a time when our people will be clamoring for these areas as they have never clamored before. Look ahead to the time when, due to the Service itself and its ideals, these places will remain intact.

I am going to close with a brief quote. A Greek philosopher once said, and you have read it before perhaps but it is worth repeating: "Life is a gift of nature, but a beautiful life is a gift of wisdom." Thank you.

Unpublished, mid-1960s

What Is Wilderness?

This editorial is Sigurd's most concise look at the meaning of wilderness. It was published at the beginning of his presidency of the Wilderness Society, and illustrates not only his longtime focus on the spiritual value of wild places but his efforts to answer those who say that wilderness preservation is elitist.

❄ ❄ ❄

THERE IS MUCH MISUNDERSTANDING as to what wilderness really is. Some think in terms of large areas, from five thousand acres to a million or more, the sort of terrain where one can get away from all evidence of civilization for a few hours or at best for days or weeks without seeing a soul. This is the traditional concept generally accepted by wilderness devotees and the public, and has given rise to the criticism that only two percent of the population, representing a select and privileged few, get to use it. The vast majority, the ninety-eight percent, say the critics, are barred from its enjoyment.

Another concept is that wilderness does not have to be large, that it can be enjoyed no matter how small it is just so it is natural and unchanged. Such little areas can be used by many more millions of people—sanctuaries close to towns and cities and completely accessible.

A great botanist once said that he got as much of a thrill out of a small patch of tundra with its mosses, lichens, and grasses as from a great stand of primitive forest; that size of area had nothing to do with it if one could see in any natural bit of country the whole dramatic story of evolution.

Both concepts are important, for it is true that small areas can provide a wilderness experience. If a bit of tundra can thrill a botanist, who is to say that others cannot derive joy from similar places. The fact remains, of course, that the larger the area the better chance there is for ecological continuity; also that in our present headlong destruction of all places of natural beauty, both large and small, we can no longer afford to quibble and argue, but should bend all our efforts toward saving wilderness wherever it is and no matter what its size or designation.

One argument seems to be overlooked because of differences of opinion as to what a wilderness experience requires. We hold up as an example of nonwilderness users the ninety-eight percent who never hike, go on pack trips, or stray from the highways or lodges. This is a fallacy, and I believe that even though they do not go into the wilderness physically, and never view it except from a comfortable lodge or a roadway, the wilderness still penetrates the consciousness much more deeply than we think. It may not be more than a brief look across a primitive valley, or a moment of meditation before some place of wildness and beauty. Whatever it is, people remember. Furthermore, the wilderness background in national parks and forests gives significance to scenic vistas and outstanding formations. In Yellowstone, the geysers and hot springs could be only scientific curiosities, but with their wilderness background their impact is immeasurable. Wilderness therefore is for everyone— the hardy hikers as well as the vast majority who have never known what it means to carry a pack. Its preservation is just as vital to one as to the other.

The preservation of wilderness is a humanitarian effort based on the knowledge that man has lived in a natural environment for some two million years and that his physiological and psychic needs come from it. No matter how urbanized or divorced from the natural man may be, within him is a powerful need for the background from which he evolved. So closely has man been identified with wilderness and so deep are his roots in the ancient rhythms, silences, and mysteries of the once unknown, that he cannot forget, and he must return often to recapture his sense of oneness with his environment. Without this opportunity to experience wilderness in his own way and wherever he may be in large wilderness regions or in minute sanctuaries he will know frustration, boredom, and unhappiness.

Wilderness preservation has to do with man's deepest inner needs and he can cut his roots to the past at his peril. In the face of our burgeoning population and industrial expansion we can draw courage from the knowledge that in the saving of places of natural beauty and wildness we are waging a battle for man's spirit. No task is more important, for the wilderness we save today will provide moral and spiritual strength and balance in a world of technology and frenzied speed. Only in a natural environment can man thrive, an environment where there are still places of beauty to go to. The effort to protect man's living space from further desecration is one of the greatest challenges of this age. Wilderness is more than camping or hiking; it is a symbol of a way of life that can nourish the spirit.

Living Wilderness, Spring 1968

A Longing for Wilderness

This introduction to a 1973 National Geographic Society book is Sigurd's longest piece on the meaning of wilderness. While it does not break new philosophical ground, the article is noteworthy for Sigurd's perspective on the history of wilderness preservation, and for its personal anecdotes. It ends in classic Sigurd Olson style, recognizing that difficult battles lay ahead, but hopeful that humankind will learn to live in harmony with the earth.

I BEGAN GUIDING CANOE PARTIES through the waterways of the Quetico-Superior country along Minnesota's border with Canada shortly after World War I. All roads ended near the little town of Ely, my home, with only an immensity of space and grandeur beyond: shimmering, island-dotted lakes reverberating to the calling of loons; rapids full of song; cliffs, forests, bogs. To me this could never change. It would always be wilderness.

But suddenly people were talking of "a road to every lake," and chambers of commerce were trumpeting the hope of developing "The Playground of a Nation." I imagined the silence of such waters as Lac la Croix and Saganaga shattered by the din of cars and motorboats, their shores lined with resorts.

That threat was followed by another: the prospect of seven hydroelectric dams with impoundments as deep as 80 feet, submerging rapids, campsites, whole river systems.

During this time I took a canoe trip along the border to see the country again before anything happened to it, a sort of voyageur's farewell to the wilderness. At Lac la Croix I climbed Warrior's Hill to get the sweep of the great historic waterway, its fleets of rugged islands with their pines leaning away from the winds, the smooth glaciated campsites, the brooding stands of timber on the mainland.

The next day I portaged around the thunder of Curtain Falls, threaded the maze of Crooked Lake, and camped on a barren isle in the very center of the swirling cauldron where the Basswood River comes plunging in. The moon was full and as always it was a place of magic until I remembered the threat. In my mind's eye I saw an apron of concrete and steel holding back the flood, the rocky gorge empty, the surging moon-drenched brilliance gone, its music stilled forever.

The following night I camped on another island above the brawling rapids of the river I had ascended, sat there in the dusk listening to the loons and the distant roar, watching the black silhouette of jagged spruce against the western sky, and I knew that man needed such beauty and solitude far more than electric power and stockholder's dividends, and that somehow the land must be saved.

The same realization had come to others. I made a canoe trip with Will Dilg, organizer of the Izaak Walton League of America, who vowed to make protection of the region a prime league objective. A Quetico-Superior Council was formed to draft a wise plan of zoning and management for the area. Men we'd guided contacted congressmen, officials, editors. Thousands who never portaged or paddled saw the effort to save the Superior National Forest and Canada's Quetico Provincial Park as a struggle to save a part of primitive North America. The tide had begun to turn when the U.S. Forest Service established the Superior Primitive Area in 1926. Known today as the Boundary

Waters Canoe Area, it is the only national forest unit dedicated to canoe travel in our National Wilderness Preservation
System.

In most of the nation untamed land had all but vanished before any action was taken to save some. The awesome fastness
that greeted the colonists of Jamestown has been whittled and
hacked, roaded, mined, suburbed, dammed. By generous reck-
oning some six percent of the old forty-eight states—less than
180,000 square miles out of more than 3 million—can today be
considered wild. The picture brightens when the emptiness of
Alaska is counted in, but there too the wilderness is shrinking.
An area estimated to equal two Rhode Islands succumbs to the
bulldozer and the cement mixer in the United States every year.
Ecologists studying the complex life chains of natural areas
often use the word "resource" when speaking of our remaining
wilderness, perhaps mindful of Aldo Leopold's observation
that "our tendency is not to call things resources until the supply runs short." Leopold was writing of this dwindling treas-
ure in 1925, a year after he had persuaded his Forest Service
superiors to establish a national wilderness—the first one—
in New Mexico.

At that time and for four decades afterward it was simply by
the stroke of an administrator's pen, always subject to a bu-
reaucratic change of heart, that wild land was rescued in the
national forests. But events were in motion which would yield
lasting results. They reached a climax in 1964 when Congress
passed the Wilderness Act, securing by law "the benefits of an
enduring resource of wilderness" not only in the forests but
also in national parks and wildlife refuges. The late Howard
Zahniser, executive director of The Wilderness Society, provided for the act a wilderness definition that soars with the spirit
of tumbling streams and virgin forests: " . . . an area where the
earth and its community of life are untrammeled by man, where
man himself is a visitor who does not remain."

Roadless and resortless, these protected lands are in most

instances beyond the grind of motors. You enter on foot—
yours or a horse's—or perhaps by canoe or on skis. Wildlife
refuges may restrict visitors to daylight hours or ban them
entirely so that fauna will not be disturbed. But for the most
part the wilderness is open and beckoning. You can hike, scale
peaks, fish the creeks for trout, hunt in the national forests and
many refuges. Or just stretch out in a meadow and watch a
hawk soar. You follow trails that may have felt the tread of
moccasins. Sometimes you come on a campsite lavishly ap-
pointed—by wilderness standards—with fireplace and grill,
or even a lean-to. But usually you make your own site with
your tent and perhaps, if downed wood is plentiful, a small
blaze to cheer the night.

Many wilderness users are family groups, sometimes trekking
with a youngster riding papoose-like in a back sling. Clubs and
outfitters sponsor group outings, usually subscribed months in
advance. Colleges utilize wilderness as a classroom, with on-
the-spot studies in ecology; sometimes these courses, borrow-
ing from Outward Bound programs, include solo hikes and
rock climbs to heighten self-awareness. The challenge of living
among woods and cascading streams has even been used in ex-
periments designed to help hospitalized mental patients shake
off defeatism and gain confidence for returning to the everyday
world.

For the tenderfoot a bit of orientation may be necessary
before wilderness yields its good tidings. Feet unaccustomed
to hiking boots and seats unacquainted with saddles may
rebel at the introduction, and the absence of a convenient
hot-dog stand may at first seem cause for alarm. But soon
even first-timers are back in the grooves of ancestral experience. Leopold once described two young canoeists who were
rapidly making the adjustment when he met them on a river
bank in Wisconsin.

What time is it? they asked. "For two days," he wrote, "they
had lived by 'suntime,' and were getting a thrill out of it. No
servant brought them meals; they got their meat out of the

river, or went without. No traffic cop whistled them off the hidden rock in the next rapids. No friendly roof kept them dry when they mis-guessed whether or not to pitch the tent. No guide showed them which camping spots offered a nightlong breeze, and which a nightlong misery of mosquitoes; which firewood made clean coals, and which only smoke." The wilderness, Leopold added, gave them "their first taste of those rewards and penalties for wise and foolish acts which every woodsman faces daily, but against which civilization has built a thousand buffers." Perhaps, he said, every youth needs an occasional outdoor adventure to learn the meaning of the freedom to make mistakes.

That freedom can be experienced in some 11 million acres of designated wilderness. The total will more than double with inclusion of areas that are well along in the designation process. Still more millions of acres will be surveyed and added to the national system in the future, and state governments are saving roadless and natural areas too. Wilderness—statutory wilderness—leaps from sea to shining sea: from the beach of Monomoy National Wildlife Refuge near Cape Cod to the islets of the Three Arch Rocks refuge off Oregon's coast. Pelican Island Wilderness in Florida musters a mere 6 acres of tangled mangroves; the Selway-Bitterroot encompasses 1,240,618 acres of Rocky Mountain high.

Increasing millions of Americans each year seek out these unspoiled lands. It may be a hidden corner where, miraculously, a mere breath of the primeval has been saved, perhaps the Great Swamp in New Jersey. A dab of sedge and slough, some stands of beech and oak, only 3,660 acres in sum, the Great Swamp Wilderness survives 25 miles from Manhattan's towers. Such places are hints of the beauty there was. People go to them for glimpses of the old America and come away refreshed.

Others crave action and horizons far beyond civilization. No tiny pockets tucked in suburbia for them! They must know the

vastness and adventure of the old frontiers. They seek the remote reaches of such little-known rivers as Alaska's Noatak,
draining the barren lands of the Arctic. They must bend against
the bite of tumplines on the portages of the Quetico-Superior,
glory in the roaring rapids of the Salmon in Idaho. They must
battle wind and storm, know hunger and hazard—and the
bond of comradeship forged on the out trails of the world.

Once in Alaska I followed a creek near the Valley of Ten
Thousand Smokes. The salmon were running, their vivid red
bodies crowding the shallows. Everywhere were signs of the
great brown bear: half-devoured fish floating downstream and
enormous bear tracks in the mud. I broke out of a tangle of
alder and saw at the end of a pool, not a hundred feet away,
a brownie with its eyes on me. We were frozen into a primeval
scene: I and this hunter at bay, face to face with the eternal
challenge, life or death. For what seemed to be two or three
hours—in truth, no more than two or three minutes—we
stared at one another. Then we went our separate ways.

From the West beckon the realms of mighty ranges: North
Cascades National Park in Washington, the John Muir Wilderness in California, the Teton Wilderness in Wyoming. Each
of these encompasses more than half a million acres of noble
spires corrugated with rill-veined valleys. One does not forget
the glory of soaring domains. I remember a morning in Alaska's
Wrangells when parting clouds revealed the grandest spectacle
of snow-capped peaks on our continent, and an autumn day in
the Never Summer country of the Colorado Rockies, with the
aspens solid gold and elk bugling in the thickets. When men
and women come down from such mountains—*their* mountains for a day, a weekend, a fortnight—they come as people
always have from lonely heights, spiritually regenerated.

There are those who feel that only in the great swamps and
flowages of the South, in the cypress stands of Georgia's Oke-
fenokee, or the mangroves of the Florida Everglades, can they

understand the true meaning of wilderness. And in a sense they are right, for it was from such watery places that terrestrial life evolved. Development has eaten out great chunks of Florida's subtropics, and thirsty cities and farms have drained much of the sustenance. Yet wild beauty remains, and flashes of it sear my mind: a rosy drift of flamingos against blue sky; three deer leaping through a silver spray of billowing saw grass; a cougar's fresh track on a muddy bank.

On the plains and prairies, remnants of grassland and the raw grandeur of the badlands lure wanderers to such places as the Wichita Mountains Wildlife Refuge in Oklahoma and Theodore Roosevelt National Memorial Park in North Dakota. Desert trails are harsh, yet men brave them willingly to roam the richly colored canyonlands of Utah or the cactus-studded fastness of Arizona. Who can deny the magic of night on that stretch of Sonoran Desert along the Mexican border known as Cabeza Prieta, under stars so bright they all but blaze? I remember the smell of greasewood and sage, and a dark valley alive with the tremulous music of coyotes. To me this unchanged land was one that night with all the great deserts of the world— and I understood why men through the ages have gone to them to gain perspective on their lives.

Mountains, deserts, swamps, forests, lakes and rivers and shores: Whatever the type, be it large or small, wilderness is balm for the tensions of the world, a place to meditate and commune with our past. In the mists of morning, ghosts speak to us of waterways flowing full and clean to the sea. When we cross the prairies it is hard to realize that until the last century they had never felt the plow, or that vast herds of buffalo roamed at will. We still have untamed space, nearly overwhelming in its magnitude, though its herds are not buffalo but caribou. Amid the glacial lakes and stunted, twisted spruce in the Alaskan taiga— the land of "little sticks"—you can hear them moving up a slope. The sound is a faint but distinctive clicking as ligaments rub against foot bones, a whisper from a virgin continent.

The pioneers who journeyed west across the plains and

mountains knew the wilderness as a place of hardship. Broken wagons, spavined oxen, and lonely graves were the waymarks of their trails. Snowbound in the Sierra Nevada, the Donner party resorted to eating dogs and hides—and human flesh when the hides gave out. Struggling across Death Valley, a party of forty-niners cursed the harsh country until, as one remembered, "it seemed as if there were not bad words enough in the language to express properly their contempt and bad opinion. . . ."

But the wilderness could be tamed, and taming it meant that a man could possess land. So the pioneers chopped and burned and plowed their way into the heart, elbowing aside and often slaughtering the Indians, not stopping until they reached the Pacific. Wild land was an inexhaustible commodity in nineteenth-century America. Homestead laws enabled more than a million families to acquire more than 248 million acres in the prairies, plains, and western mountains. Railroads were granted 150 million acres, war veterans 61 million, the states more than 300 million for such purposes as supporting schools and building wagon roads and canals.

Out of their desperate years the settlers knew a fierce pride of accomplishment. The wilderness discarded Old World notions of aristocracy; on the frontier a man proved himself in the crucible of survival. In time the pioneers developed a sense of continental belonging to the land, a loyalty welded of hope and struggle. The wilderness molded them—and us—as a people. "American democracy . . . was not carried in the *[Susan] Constant* to Virginia, nor in the *Mayflower* to Plymouth," wrote historian Frederick Jackson Turner. "It came out of the American forest, and it gained new strength each time it touched a new frontier." But in the very process of conquering the wilds, the pioneers were chopping their spiritual roots.

The world we face now is a strange one, the great silences replaced with clamor, the hearts of our cities garish with blinking neon and foul with the stench of pollution. We look at the

slums, at the never-ending traffic, the shrinking space and growing ugliness, and are appalled. Is this, we ask, what our forebears
struggled for? Is this the great American dream?

We enjoy comforts never known before, but they are not
enough; somehow, someway, we must make contact with naturalness, the source of all life. The frontiers are still too close to
forget and the memory of wilderness goes far back into the eons
when man lived close to the earth and was in tune with the ancient rhythms. We still listen to the song of the wilderness and
long for a land we have lost. Civilization has not changed emotional needs which were ours long before it arose. This is the
reason for the hunger, this the true meaning of wilderness and
the search of moderns for places where they can know it again.
The battle to save the last remnants is not only a struggle for
freedom and beauty, but for the spirit of man in a world that
seems to have lost its balance and perspective.

"Something will have gone out of us as a people if we ever
let the remaining wilderness be destroyed," the author Wallace
Stegner warned some years ago, "if we permit the last virgin
forests to be turned into comic books and plastic cigarette cases;
if we drive the few remaining members of the wild species into
zoos or to extinction; if we pollute the last clear air and dirty
the last clean streams and push our paved roads through the
last of the silence. . . . The reassurance that it is still there is
good for our spiritual health even if we never once in 10 years
set foot in it."

Though the yearning spirit in us often obscures them, there
also are practical reasons for saving what's left of wilderness.
Man is a manipulator of nature—more so now than ever as he
seeks by pesticides, defoliants, fertilizers, irrigation schemes, and
cloud-seeding chemicals to grow food and fiber with heightened
efficiency. But he is far from a complete understanding of the
processes he manipulates. In the complex ecosystems of natural
domains he has a laboratory in which to study the interaction
of species, environmental trends, evolution. And in undisturbed
flora and fauna he has a storehouse of genetic diversity the future
may prize.

As early as the 1830s the frontier artist George Catlin suggested that the government create a preserve where the world
in ages to come could view the wild freshness of nature. At
midcentury the rustic philosopher of Walden, Henry David
Thoreau, was advocating much the same thing. "In Wildness
is the preservation of the World," he declared; why should not
some be saved for "our own true recreation"?

Such men were setting the stage for John Muir. How best to
type this bearded wilderness fanatic? Incorrigible wanderer, in-
ventor, naturalist—he was all three. But with a pen in his hand
he was something more: a poet on a crusade. Writing, he once
grumbled, is "like the life of a glacier, one eternal grind." But
grind he did: nine books, hundreds of newspaper and magazine
articles, letters. As no man had before, Muir infected Americans
with the joy of nature and alerted them to the dangers of mind-
less exploitation.

"Climb the mountains and get their good tidings," he ex-
horted. "Nature's peace will flow into you as sunshine flows
into trees." He campaigned to save Yosemite, the mountains
of all the West, the glaciers, fiords, and forests of Alaska. Do-
mestic sheep grazing the fragile high country he condemned as
"hoofed locusts." He fought for trees, especially the sequoias.
"It took more than 3,000 years to make some of the trees in
these western woods . . ." he once wrote. "Through all the wonderful, eventful centuries since Christ's time—and long before
that—God has cared for these trees . . . but he cannot save them
from fools. Only Uncle Sam can do that."

Muir and the handful of men who thought as he did arrived
on the scene at a desperate time. "The Age of Extermination,"
naturalists have called the last half of the nineteenth century, an
era of rampant and ghastly abuse of both wildlife and landscape.
Eastern forests were largely devastated and lumbermen were
sawing away at the public lands of the West. In the Deep South
spoonbills, flamingos, ibises, egrets, and other plume birds were
being blunderbussed to provide trimmings for milady's hats.
Hunters were blasting to oblivion the passenger pigeon, once

the most numerous American bird. Buffalo were gunned down
by the millions.

But the country had been alerted. Responsible public ser-
vants began to act. Presidents Benjamin Harrison and Grover
Cleveland created the first forest reserves from public lands in
the 1890s. "Lockout!" shouted loggers and stockmen. But the
reserves remained. Gifford Pinchot, America's first native-born
professional forester—he had studied silviculture in Europe—
argued that forests should be "managed" for the national good.
"Managed" meant trees could be harvested, but the principal
manager would be the government. Reforestation would be
an important element. It was thus that he advised his friend,
President Theodore Roosevelt.

Pinchot's utilitarian approach disappointed Muir, who
saw a canopy of conifers as a temple. But as T. R.'s counsel
the forester achieved much for which Muir's modern disciples
are grateful; Roosevelt built the forest reserves to 172 million
acres, including many of the most magnificent tracts which
afford us pleasure today. That was not the only signal achieve-
ment of this conservation-minded president. Naturalist and
hunter, he "gave the vanishing birds and animals the benefit
of every doubt," as a zoologist noted, creating the first national wildlife refuge on Florida's Pelican Island in 1903 and later
fifty others. He also set aside eighteen areas of historic or natural interest, including Grand Canyon, the Petrified Forest, and
Muir Woods.

A wilderness, Aldo Leopold wrote in 1921, when he was an
assistant district forester in the Southwest, should be "big
enough to absorb a two weeks' pack trip." It should be devoid
of "roads, artificial trails, cottages, or other works of man." In
1919 Leopold had met a fellow Iowan, Arthur Carhart, a landscape architect employed as the Forest Service's first fulltime
recreation engineer. Carhart described his own efforts to rescue
313-acre Trappers Lake in the White River National Forest in
Colorado. Ordered to execute a design for siting summer cabins,

Carhart argued—successfully, as it turned out—that houses and a road would destroy the beauty. He had seen the Quetico-Superior and thought it also should be saved, and a few years later was involved there in the fight to keep out roads.

Leopold had his eye on a fine wilderness in the Gila National Forest in New Mexico—a region of piñon and ponderosa pines, box canyons, and peaks soaring beyond 10,000 feet. Deer and turkey were abundant. "Report on Proposed Wilderness Area" is the title of a memorandum he submitted in 1922. It declared:

"Object. To preserve at least one place in the Southwest where pack trips shall be the 'dominant play.' . . .

"Function. A 'National Hunting Ground' is the one form of recreation which has not been provided for or recognized by the federal government. . . ."

Leopold had spent his boyhood hunting and fishing along the Mississippi River, and well into manhood the hunter's instinct pulsed in his veins. He once applauded the "splendid progress" of a campaign to rid New Mexico of such predators as wolves and mountain lions. The evidence, however, is that Leopold did not view designated wilderness in the single dimension of sport. Save only the tilling of the soil, no outdoor activity "bends and molds the human character like wilderness travel," he wrote in the American Forestry Association's magazine in the 1920s. "Would we rather have the few paltry dollars that could be extracted from our remaining wild places than the human values they can render in their wild condition?" He urged support for preservation of tracts in both forests and national parks.

On June 3, 1924, a Gila Wilderness Area of 750,000 acres was created in a memorandum signed by the Southwest district forester. Two years later the chief of the Forest Service urged other administrators to designate wild lands, and in 1929 wilderness preservation was adopted as official Forest Service policy. In later years the Gila's boundaries would contract as foresters bowed to local pressures for mining, logging, and highway rights-of-way. But something very profound in the history of preservation had happened there among the box canyons and pines.

Eventually Leopold traded the rifle for the bow and arrow, and then those for the notebook, acquiring stature as a conservationist and ecologist. Thousands were influenced toward the rescue of the land and its resources by the compact but powerful essays in his slim classic, *A Sand County Almanac*. Once when we were discussing my own studies of wolves in Minnesota I chided him for having been an advocate of extermination. "We've come a long way since then," he answered. Just how far Leopold showed in his magnificent essay, "Thinking Like a Mountain," about the shooting of a she-wolf on a Southwestern peak. I quoted to him that day a paragraph from the essay, as he closed his eyes and remembered:

"We reached the old wolf in time to watch a fierce green fire dying in her eyes. I realized then, and have known ever since, that there was something new to me in those eyes—something known only to her and to the mountain. I was young then, and full of trigger-itch; I thought that because fewer wolves meant more deer, that no wolves would mean hunters' paradise. But after seeing the green fire die, I sensed that neither the wolf nor the mountain agreed with such a view."

A fellow conservationist of the 1930s dubbed Robert Marshall "the most efficient weapon of preservation in existence." He approached everything with vigor—most of all, wild land. Marshall thought nothing of backpacking 40 or 50 miles a day, usually wearing tennis shoes, and several times paced off an incredible 70. At the end of one of those days he declared: "A man must work for his wilderness enjoyment. Only when he's hungry, thirsty, and dog-tired can he really know what it means." With Bob Marshall involved, there was no chance the fledgling wilderness movement would be neglected.

We made a trip together in the Boundary Waters Canoe Area when he was the Forest Service's chief of recreation. "We'll go in paddling and come out the same way, no launches, no airplanes, no mechanized transportation of any kind," he had written me. "I want to see the country as the voyageurs saw it, and travel it as they." The trip was all adventure and delight—or nearly so. Once we came on a portage route which had been straightened by the Civilian Conservation Corps. "A cellophane trail," Marshall called it in disgust. "Portages are sacred. We must leave them alone. There are plenty of straight trails in America." He felt that campsites used by Indians and frontiersmen were best; they had "atmosphere and feeling."

In 1931 Marshall returned from a 13-month adventure in the Alaskan Arctic overflowing with zeal. He rained pleas for safeguarding wild land upon officials in Washington. Several of our greatest forest wildernesses—the Pasayten and the Three Sisters in the Cascades, the Selway-Bitterroot in the Rockies, to name but three—were established while his powerful voice sounded in the Capital. As a Forest Service official he won stricter regulations for the protection of wilderness tracts; outside the government he helped found The Wilderness Society, today one of the strongest voices for preservation.

"We can never have enough of Nature," Thoreau wrote. "We must be refreshed by the sight of inexhaustible vigor, vast and Titanic features. . . ." Thoreau spoke for Marshall and for all the unheralded citizens who continued the fight to save parts of the earth inviolate. All endured heartbreak and frustration while seeking to arouse a bureaucracy or a public dominated by the frontier view of land and the belief that the local economy mattered more than a gift of ages.

I was drawn inevitably to other areas where wilderness and beauty were threatened. One day I stood with friends on the beach of Indiana Dunes watching the whitecaps of Lake Michigan march in from the north. For thousands of years the winds had howled down that 300-mile stretch of water, building the beach and hurling its sands onto the giant living dunes behind it. Again the old question: Must open space and the natural legacy of millenniums always be sacrificed? As we looked across at the twinkling lights of Chicago and the blood-red sky above the blast furnaces of Gary, the answer was the same as it had been in the Quetico-Superior long before: "People need glimpses of the primeval for the good of their souls. They need it far more than another industrial complex."

At Point Reyes, a short ride north of San Francisco's Golden Gate, I walked with other friends one day when the Pacific was blue and the air rich with the scent of laurel, lilac, and lupine. We climbed a promontory and looked down on the roaring surf, alive with glistening sea lions. This was the Point Reyes that Drake and Spanish explorers had sighted long before the gold rush. It was hard to believe that in a few years suburbia would engulf it. I already knew the battle slogans: People or Scenery; Ghettos or Homes; Taxes or Poverty. In time most of Point Reyes, like the Indiana dunes, became a national shoreline, but opponents still skirmish over how much of the park land should be preserved in the wilderness system.

I stood among the redwoods as chain saws felled the giant trees; in Dinosaur National Monument in Utah and Colorado when a dam threatened not only the canyons but the sanctity of the entire national park system; in the forests of the Olympics; on Cape Cod National Seashore. Always the thin rank of wilderness proponents manned the ramparts. And emerging everywhere was a dream of giving wild places, long embattled, surcease and solid protection—not through an order from a government department, too easily rescinded, but by the force of law.

So, the wilderness champions banded together—thousands of individuals and members of such organizations as The Wilderness Society, the Izaak Walton League, and the Sierra Club—and asked Congress for help. Their battle was not won easily; it meant redirecting a nation's way of thinking. Mining companies opposed the wilderness concept, one spokesman even charging that it played into the hands of the Soviet Union. Sheepmen condemned wilderness as a breeding ground for predators. Cattlemen argued that "ever-increasing pleasure areas" would result in carelessly set fires. The parent bodies of the three federal agencies whose lands would be involved—the Department of Agriculture for the Forest Service, the Department of the Interior for the National Park Service, and the Fish and Wildlife Service—declared that the proposed legislation would interfere with their management activities. Eight years passed from the introduction of the first bill until the Wilderness Act cleared Congress and was signed by President Lyndon B. Johnson on September 3, 1964.

"A compromise among human beings with conflicting desires," a Wilderness Society worker characterized the act. Bowing to mining interests, it permitted prospecting to continue in national forest wildernesses until the end of 1983. Cattlemen and shepherds would still be able to graze their herds in wilderness meadows (though officials have reduced the number of grazing permits). The ban against motorized equipment was skewed to permit a few "established" practices: Planes could continue to land hunters and hikers deep within the Selway-Bitterroot, for instance, and motorboats still could ply parts of the Boundary Waters Canoe Area.

But there was, at last, a National Wilderness Preservation System, composed of lands that retained their "primeval character and influence, without permanent improvements or human habitation . . . with the imprint of man's work substantially unnoticeable." A wilderness was further defined as having "outstanding opportunities for solitude or a primitive and unconfined type of recreation"; it must be at least 5,000 acres or, if smaller (as are a number of wildlife refuges), capable of being preserved in "an unimpaired condition." Areas that won the designation would continue to be managed by their respective agency landlords, but the rules of the act would apply: no roads, power lines, dams, resorts, logging.

President Johnson's signature put into the system that day in 1964 more than 9 million acres which the Forest Service had been administratively protecting, beginning with Leopold's Gila. These 54 tracts included the Boundary Waters Canoe Area and lands the administrators had classified before 1964 as "wilderness" (areas of 100,000 acres or more) or "wild" (between 5,000 and 100,000 acres). Also in the national forests in 1964 were 34 parcels, 5.4 million acres in sum, called "primitive." These consisted of lands that were candidates for upgrading to "wilderness" or "wild" status, though some also were marked by fire roads and other works of man. For the most part they were being protected from further encroachment so that some day the parts predominantly valuable for wilderness could be elevated on the scale. The act required that the national forest Primitive Areas now be reviewed for inclusion in the wilderness system, subject, as all new wildernesses would be, to congressional approval.

In the national parks all roadless areas of 5,000 acres or more were to be reviewed, and in the wildlife refuges all roadless areas of that size as well as roadless islands. The backcountry parts of parks and monuments in particular had been held in a natural state; logging had been banned in all of them, mining in all but four units. The refuges, though less rigidly protected (they are open to mineral leasing), also contained undeveloped lands. Within these two systems more than 175 parks and refuges have been identified for wilderness consideration.

Beyond its definition and guidelines, the Wilderness Act's most important feature is a provision for citizen involvement. In preparing recommendations to the President on each candidate area, officials must publicize the proposals and invite public expression. Of course this procedure also allows opponents of wilderness to be heard. But the advocates nearly always outnumber the other side by lopsided margins. For example, the Forest Service's wilderness plan for the Gore Range–Eagles Nest Primitive Area in Colorado generated nearly 19,000 written responses—letters, postcards, and petition signatures—and elicited statements at hearings from 213 persons. These last represented groups as diverse as the American Legion, the Denver Audubon Society, and a high school biology club. By far the largest response was registered in favor not of the Forest Service's plan for a 72,000-acre wilderness but of one larger by more than two-thirds—a resounding plea for preservation.

Years, perhaps decades, will pass before the task of protecting wilderness is complete. Ten years were allowed for the agencies to review potential areas; other years will go by as Congress ponders their recommendations, perhaps expanding some boundaries and shrinking others as local pressures come into play. The Alaskan backcountry may someday provide enormous new areas; the Alaska Native Claims Settlement Act authorizes the allocation of some 80 million acres for national parks, refuges, forests, and wild and scenic rivers.

Meanwhile, the Wilderness Act's silence on other land of great potential—especially the 56 million acres of roadless but undesignated lands in the national forests—has triggered numerous disputes. Only a fifth of these so-called "de facto" areas have so far been proposed for wilderness study; conservationists hope to see all the roadless lands reviewed under the Wilderness Act procedures. Other disputes simmer over the drawing of wilderness boundaries in some of the national parks and refuges, and still others over the future of public lands held by the Bureau of Land Management in the West. Though not subject to the act, the Bureau has selected several areas, mainly in the canyonlands, to be administratively kept as wild land; some 60 others are under review.

And what should be done with forests that once, perhaps half a century ago, heard the ring of axes and breathed the smoke of frontier cabins? The question has raged east of the Mississippi, where most of the national forests were once logged.

There's a special charm for me in places that have reverted from farm to forest, as in much of the Appalachians. Of course the enormous chestnuts are gone, victims of blight, and along with them virgin pines and hemlocks that towered in the silence. But the generous rain of the eastern mountains is a potent restorative. And so one now finds in cut-over forests thriving stands of hardwoods, spruce, fir, and white pine, conjuring a sense of wildness as the predecessor forest must have to settlers. Then, without warning, you come on an old stone wall, a chimney of fieldstone, a lilac bush growing wild. Relics of our heritage, they are a poignant dowry bestowed upon the land, giving a deeper meaning to wilderness. But as the Forest Service has interpreted the Wilderness Act, such places are trammeled.

To officials besieged with mail from conservationists, or listening to hundreds testifying at hearings, it must often seem that wilderness lovers want the whole continent restored. What they really want is *enough* wilderness—whatever the sum may be, and no one can know it yet—to satisfy the millions who seek its pleasures.

Were John Muir to return today to his beloved High Sierra in peak season, one writer has noted, he would meet a ranger who might instruct him thus: "Bullfrog and Timberline Lakes are closed to camping and grazing. In the Evolution Basin and at Kearsarge Lakes wood fires are prohibited. You can stay only one night at Paradise Valley, Woods Creek, Rae Lakes, Kearsarge Lakes, Charlotte Lakes, Sixty Lakes Basin, Junction Meadow, and Bubbs Creek. Oh, and please remember to camp at least 100 feet away from lakes and streams. Thank you and have a good trip." Such a thicket of restrictions has become necessary in many areas to protect vegetation from trampling, streams from pollution, and solitude from crowds. In an ever-growing list of park and forest wildernesses, campers must obtain a permit to spend the night. Demand has simply outstripped supply.

Many national forest wildernesses were created in areas of little value for timber—too remote for profitable logging, too high or too dry to yield more than scrub. As the yearning for wilderness grows, the Forest Service responds that it must provide other goods and services also. A quarter of the nation's lumber and plywood is cut on its lands; car and trailer campers must be considered; there is more pressure for ski areas and resorts. No national policies sort out the priorities. So our wilderness system continues in yeasty ferment, and the ideal is far away.

A few years ago I looked out over an expanse of wild country from Sherman Pass, high over the Kern River in Sequoia National Forest. The trail had led upward from sagebrush and rabbit brush, up through piñons and scrub oak, with patches of Indian paintbrush flaming along the way. At the top the trees were wind-tortured, scraggly, frayed—seemingly as old as the rocks. I caught the blue flash of a Steller's jay, heard the faint nasal tones of nuthatches. A buzzard wheeled overhead, coasting the currents. Far to the north rose the mass of Mount Whitney, brooding over the ancestral home of the famous golden trout.

It saddened me to learn later that loggers had set upon this great realm and that a road was inching across the mountains, even through Sherman Pass. An opportunity was lost here for relieving some of the pressure on other Sierra wildernesses, and as the saws and tractors ripped across the Kern Plateau, a bit more of the heart and soul of America, of the wilderness that shaped us, was destroyed.

The millions who quest after the peace and glory of wild places must, like their compatriots in decades past, live with such disappointments—and fight on. The Wilderness Act is a foundation, a great victory for the land, a lode of law which will reward future struggles with victories that are not fleeting. There is hope, too, in the deepening awareness that man cannot forever exploit resources with the abandon of a pioneer in a boundless domain. Man is slowly learning to live in harmony with the earth, using his vast technology to right past wrongs, to clean despoiled rivers and poisoned air. "It has never been man's gift to make wildernesses," Wallace Stegner observed. "But he can make deserts, and has." The choice is ours. I have faith that the wild places will win out.

In *Wilderness U.S.A.* (Washington, D.C.:
National Geographic Society, 1973)

Writings by Sigurd F. Olson

BOOKS

Olson's books are listed in chronological order. Posthumous collections of his writings are included.

The Singing Wilderness. New York: Alfred A. Knopf, 1956. Reprint, Minneapolis: University of Minnesota Press, 1997.

Listening Point. New York: Alfred A. Knopf, 1958. Reprint, Minneapolis: University of Minnesota Press, 1997.

The Lonely Land. New York: Alfred A. Knopf, 1961. Reprint, Minneapolis: University of Minnesota Press, 1997.

Runes of the North. New York: Alfred A. Knopf, 1963. Reprint, Minneapolis: University of Minnesota Press, 1997.

Open Horizons. New York: Alfred A. Knopf, 1969. Reprint, Minneapolis: University of Minnesota Press, 1998.

The Hidden Forest. New York: Viking Press, 1969.

Wilderness Days. New York: Alfred A. Knopf, 1972.

Reflections from the North Country. New York: Alfred A. Knopf, 1976. Reprint, Minneapolis: University of Minnesota Press, 1998.

Of Time and Place. New York: Alfred A. Knopf, 1982. Reprint, Minneapolis: University of Minnesota Press, 1998.

Songs of the North. Howard Frank Mosher, ed. Penguin Nature Library. New York: Penguin Books, 1987.

The Collected Works of Sigurd F. Olson: The Early Writings, 1921–1934. Mike Link, ed. Introduction by Robert Keith Olson. Stillwater, Minn.: Voyageur Press, 1988.

The Collected Works of Sigurd F. Olson: The College Years, 1935–1944.
Mike Link, ed. Introduction by Jim Klobuchar. Stillwater,
Minn.: Voyageur Press, 1990.

ARTICLES AND BOOK CHAPTERS

This section lists Olson's magazine and newspaper articles and book
chapters, arranged in chronological order. Speeches that were revised
for publication are included in this section. (Speeches published in
conference proceedings follow in a separate section.) The following
are not included: book excerpts, published letters to the editor, and
titles of Olson's "America Out of Doors" syndicated newspaper column, which was published in a few American newspapers between
1941 and 1944.

1920s

"Canoe Tourist Finds Joys of the Great Outdoors through the Vast
Watered Wilderness of the North." *Milwaukee Journal,* July 31,
1921. (This article also was printed about the same time in the
Nashwauk (Minn.) Herald under the title "Describes Cruise
Thru the Woods," and indeed may have appeared there first. The
Olson family found a clipping of the article in 1999; it is undated,
but the issue number of 28 appears, indicating a likely mid-July
time frame. Sigurd would have been somewhat disappointed,
however, because there was no byline. The *Milwaukee Journal*
article is the first to list his name as the writer.)
"Fishin' Jewelry." *Field and Stream,* November 1927.
"Snow Wings." *Boys' Life,* March 1928.
"Reflections of a Guide." *Field and Stream,* June 1928.

1930s

"Duck Heaven." *Outdoor Life,* October 1930.
"Confessions of a Duck Hunter." *Sports Afield,* October 1930.
"Stag Pants Galahads." *Sports Afield,* November 1930.
"The Poison Trail." *Sports Afield,* December 1930.
"Spring Fever." *Sports Afield,* April 1931.
"The Blue-Bills Are Coming!" *Sports Afield,* October 1931.
"Papette." *Sports Afield,* January and February 1932.
"Search for the Wild." *Sports Afield,* May and June 1932.
"Fortune at Lac La Croix." *Sports Afield,* September and October 1932.

"Trail's End." *Sports Afield,* October 1933.

"Roads or Planes in the Superior." *Minnesota Waltonian,* April 1934.

"A New Policy Needed for the Superior." *Minnesota Conservationist,* May 1934.

"Cruising in the Arrowhead." *Outdoors,* May 1934.

"The Evolution of a Canoe Country." *Minnesota Conservationist,* May 1935.

"Sere, Climax and Influent Animals with Special Reference to the Transcontinental Coniferous Forest of North America." (Coauthored with Victor E. Shelford.) *Ecology,* July 1935.

"The Romance of Portages." *Minnesota Conservationist,* April 1936.

"Let's Go Exploring." *Field and Stream,* June 1937.

"Organization and Range of the Pack." *Ecology,* January 1938.

"Taking Us, Dad?" *Field and Stream,* January 1938.

"A Study in Predatory Relationship with Particular Reference to the Wolf." *Scientific Monthly,* April 1938.

"Wilderness Areas." *Sports Afield,* August 1938.

"Why Wilderness?" *American Forests,* September 1938.

"Mallards Are Different." *Field and Stream,* November 1938.

"The Immortals of Argo." *Sports Afield,* July 1939.

"Mallards of Back Bay." *Sports Afield,* October 1939.

1940s

"Fireside Pictures." *Field and Stream,* March 1940.

"The Last Mallard." *Sports Afield,* November 1940.

"What! No Bass?" *Field and Stream,* January 1941.

"The Bohemians." *Minneapolis Star-Journal,* March 23, 1941.

"First Spring Flower." *Minneapolis Star-Journal,* March 30, 1941.

"Easter on the Prairie." *Minneapolis Star-Journal,* April 13, 1941.

"Spring Morning." *Minneapolis Star-Journal,* April 20, 1941.

"The Iron Mine." *Minneapolis Star-Journal,* April 27, 1941.

"Balm of Gilead." *Minneapolis Star-Journal,* May 4, 1941.

"Opening Day." *Minneapolis Star-Journal,* May 11, 1941.

"The Three Spruces." *Minneapolis Star-Journal,* May 18, 1941.

"Prairie Pool." *Minneapolis Star-Journal,* May 25, 1941.

"Swan Song." *Minneapolis Star-Journal,* June 1, 1941.

"The Call of the Flock." *Minneapolis Star-Journal,* June 8, 1941.

"Wilderness Short Cuts." *Sports Afield,* 1942 Fishing Annual.

"War Comes to the Quetico." *Sports Afield,* February 1942.

"Wilderness Again on Trial." *Outdoor America,* May–June 1942.

"Quetico-Superior Wilderness International and Unique." *Living Wilderness,* December 1942.

"Packs and Paddles." *Sports Afield,* 1943 Fishing Annual.

"Gold in Them Hills." *Sports Afield,* July 1944.

"The Spring Hole." *Outdoor Life,* September 1944.

"I'm a Jump Shooter." *Sports Afield,* October 1944.

"Shift of the Wind." *Sports Afield,* December 1944.

"Wilderness Manners." *Sports Afield,* May 1945.

"The Purist." *Conservation Volunteer,* May–June 1945.

"Flying In." *Sports Afield,* September 1945.

"The Gremlins of Wind Bay." *Sports Afield,* November 1945.

"Spawning of the Eelpout." *Conservation Volunteer,* January–February 1946.

"We Need Wilderness." *National Parks Magazine,* January–March 1946. Reprinted in condensed form in *Plants and Gardens,* Winter 1946.

"On Not Trimming Trees." *Conservation Volunteer,* March–April 1946.

"Canoeing for Sport." *The Outdoorsman,* February 1948.

"Let's Finish What We Started." *Outdoor America,* February 1948.

"Moon Magic." *Sports Afield,* February 1948.

"Veterans Named." *Christian Science Monitor,* March 22, 1948.

"Quetico-Superior Elegy." *Living Wilderness,* Spring 1948.

"Quetico-Superior Challenge." *Sports Afield,* May 1948.

"Wings over the Wilderness." *American Forests,* June 1948.

"Voyageur's Return." *Nature Magazine,* June–July 1948.

"The Know-How in Camping." *The Outdoorsman,* August 1948.

"The Preservation of Wilderness." *Living Wilderness,* Autumn 1948.

"Rainbow Forty." *Toronto Star Weekly,* October 2, 1948.

"Spawning of the Pike." *Conservation Volunteer,* January–February 1949.

"Battle for a Wilderness." *Forest and Outdoors,* March 1949.

"Frog Chorus." *Conservation Volunteer,* April 1949.

"Canadians Urge International Forest." *Ely Miner,* September 1, 1949.

"Voyageurs' Country." *National Home Monthly,* October 1949.

"Swift as the Wild Goose Flies." *National Parks Magazine,* October–December 1949.

1950s

"A Victory for Wilderness!" *Outdoor America,* January 1950.

"Late Frontier Quetico-Superior." *American Heritage,* Spring 1950.

"Wilderness Victory." *National Parks Magazine*, April–June 1950.
"Airplane Ban Goes into Effect." *Outdoor America*, January–February 1951.
"Canoe Country." *North Country*, Spring 1951.
"The Drummer." *North Country*, Spring 1951.
"Spring Fever." *North Country*, Spring 1951.
"Calling of the Loon." *North Country*, Summer 1951.
"Grand Portage Dedication." *North Country*, Summer 1951.
"Orchids of the North." *North Country*, Summer 1951.
"The Quetico-Superior Wilderness Laboratory." *Science Teacher*, November 1951.
"The Rainy Lake Pollution Problem." *Outdoor America*, November–December 1951.
"The Big Snow." *Gopher Historian*, January 1953.
"Voyageur's Country: The Story of the Quetico-Superior Country." *Wilson Bulletin*, March 1953.
"Conservation and Citizenship." *Gopher Historian*, April 1953.
"Airplanes to Wilderness." *Living Wilderness*, Spring 1953.
"Wilderness and the Flambeau." *Living Wilderness*, Spring 1953.
"Let's Take a Canoe Trip." *Recreation*, February 1954.
"The Challenge of Our National Parks." *National Parks Magazine*, April–June 1954.
"The Intangible Values in Nature Protection." *National Parks Magazine*, July–September 1954.
"Canoe Country Manners." *Duluth News Tribune*, September 5, 1954.
"Right Should Prevail." *Outdoor America*, July–August 1955.
"This Is No Little Bird Book." *Living Wilderness*, Winter–Spring 1955–56.
"The Association's First Objective." *National Parks Magazine*, January–March 1956.
"A U.S. Comment." *American Forests*, February 1956.
"The Association's Second Objective." *National Parks Magazine*, April–June 1956.
"The Association's Third Objective." *National Parks Magazine*, July–September 1956.
"The Association's Fourth Objective." *National Parks Magazine*, October–December 1956.
"Outlaw Country." *True*, February 1957.
"Our Need of Breathing Space." In Henry Jarrett, ed., *Perspectives on Conservation*. Baltimore: Johns Hopkins, 1958.

"Winning a Wilderness." *Naturalist,* Winter 1958.
"Leisure Time: Man's Key to Self Realization—The Out-of-Doors."
   Minnesota Journal of Education, April 1958.
"The Quetico-Superior." *Outdoor America,* May 1958.
"Thanksgiving: More than a Holiday." *Outdoor America,* November
   1958.
"Of Worms and Fishermen." *Outdoor America,* April 1959.
"Beauty Belongs to All." *Naturalist,* Fall 1959.
"Wilderness Manners." *Forest and Outdoors,* October 1959.
"Woodsmen's Skill for the Wild." *Living Wilderness,* Winter 1959–60.

1960s through 1982

"Winning a Wilderness." *Outdoor America,* June 1960.
"Some New Books in Review: Portage into the Past." *Minnesota
   History,* March 1961.
"Explorers." *Naturalist,* Winter 1961.
"The Meaning of the National Parks." In Victor H. Cahalane, ed.,
   National Parks: A World Need. New York: American Committee
   for International Wild Life Protection, Special Publication
   No. 14, 1962.
"The Wilderness Concept." *The Ames Forester,* 1962 annual.
"Six Decades of Progress." *American Forests,* October 1962.
"Sam Campbell, Philosopher of the Forest." *American Forests,*
   October 1962.
"Relics from the Rapids." *National Geographic,* September 1963.
"Wilderness Preservation." *Naturalist,* Winter 1964.
"Voyageur's Autumn." *Boys' Life,* November 1964.
"Minnesota's Proposed National Park." *Naturalist,* Spring 1965.
"Skindiving for Treasures of the Past." *Ford Times,* April 1965.
"Natural Resource Readings: A Wilderness Bill of Rights." *Journal of
   Soil and Water Conservation,* March–April 1966.
"Wilderness Canoe Country: Minnesota's Greatest Recreational
   Asset." *Naturalist,* Spring 1967.
"What Is Wilderness?" *Living Wilderness,* Spring 1968.
"A Certain Kind of Man." *The Beaver,* Autumn 1968.
"A Tribute to F. L. Jaques." *Naturalist,* Spring 1970.
"Wilderness Challenge." *Living Wilderness,* Summer 1970.
"Wilderness Besieged: The Canoe Country of Minnesota." *Audubon,*
   July 1970.

"The Values of Voyageurs National Park." *Minnesota Conservation Volunteer,* May–June 1971.
"Alaska: Land of Scenic Grandeur." *Living Wilderness,* Winter 1971–72.
"What of Beautiful Minnesota?" In *Century 2: In Perspective.* Minneapolis: Northwestern National Bank, 1972.
"A Longing for Wilderness." In Seymour L. Fishbein, ed., *Wilderness U.S.A.* Washington, D.C.: National Geographic Society, 1973.
"A Giant Step North." *The Rotarian,* March 1974.
"Wild Islands of the Shield." *Naturalist,* Summer 1975.
"Caribou Creek." *Audubon,* March 1982.

SPEECHES PUBLISHED IN CONFERENCE PROCEEDINGS

"Air Space Reservations over Wilderness." Presented in March 1949, this speech is in *Transactions, 14th North American Wildlife Conference.* Washington, D.C.: Wildlife Management Institute, 1949.
"Conservation Appeal." Presented in March 1950, this speech is in *Transactions, 15th North American Wildlife Conference.* Washington, D.C.: Wildlife Management Institute, 1950.
"Summarization of the Sixteenth North American Wildlife Conference." Presented in March 1951, this speech is in *Transactions, 16th North American Wildlife Conference.* Washington, D.C.: Wildlife Management Institute, 1951.
"Our Public Lands: Shall the Public Abdicate Control?" Presented in March 1958, this speech is in *Transactions, 23rd North American Wildlife Conference.* Washington, D.C.: Wildlife Management Institute, 1958.
"The Spiritual Aspects of Wilderness." Olson gave this talk in April 1961 at the 7th Biennial Wilderness Conference, held in San Francisco. It is published in David Brower, ed., *Wilderness: America's Living Heritage.* San Francisco: Sierra Club, 1961.
"A Philosophical Concept." Olson gave this talk in July 1962 during the First World Conference on National Parks, held in Seattle. It is included in Alexander B. Adams, ed., *First World Conference on National Parks.* Washington, D.C., 1964.
"The Spiritual Need." Olson gave this talk in April 1965 at the 9th Biennial Wilderness Conference, held in San Francisco. It is published in Bruce M. Kilgore, ed., *Wilderness in a Changing World.* San Francisco: Sierra Club, 1966.

"From the Friday Afternoon Discussion." This technically is not a
speech, but there are some interesting comments from Olson
in this reprinted discussion that took place during the 10th
Wilderness Conference in San Francisco in April 1967. It is
published in Maxine E. McCloskey and James P. Gilligan, ed.,
Wilderness and the Quality of Life. San Francisco: Sierra Club,
1969.

Index

The abbreviation SFO is used to indicate Sigurd F. Olson.

SIGURD F. OLSON (1899–1982) was one of the greatest environmentalists of the twentieth century. A conservation activist and popular writer, he introduced a generation of Americans to the importance of wilderness. He served as president of the Wilderness Society and the National Parks Association and as a consultant to the federal government on wilderness preservation and ecological problems. He earned many honors, including the highest possible recognition from the Sierra Club, National Wildlife Federation, and Izaak Walton League.

His books include *The Singing Wilderness* (1956), *Listening Point* (1958), *The Lonely Land* (1961), *Runes of the North* (1963), *Open Horizons* (1969), *The Hidden Forest* (1969), *Wilderness Days* (1972), *Reflections from the North Country* (1976), and *Of Time and Place* (1982). These works created a new genre of nature writing that was infused with beauty and respect for our nation's wild places. He received the John Burroughs Medal, the highest honor in nature writing, and frequently appeared on best-seller lists across the nation.

For most of his life, he lived and worked in Ely, Minnesota, gateway to the Quetico-Superior region.

DAVID BACKES is professor of journalism and mass communication at the University of Wisconsin–Milwaukee. His book *A Wilderness Within: The Life of Sigurd F. Olson* (Minnesota, 1997) won the 1998 Small Press Book Award for best biography. He is also the author of *Canoe Country: An Embattled Wilderness* and *The Wilderness Companion*.